PACIFIC OCEAN ROUTE OF THE CAIRO III

Scale of miles

0   400   800

Adrift
Jan. 25

Clipperton
Island

Puntarenas,
Costa Rica

Galapagos Islands

110°   100°   90°   80°

FIVE AGAINST THE SEA

FIVE AGAINST THE SEA

A True Story of Courage and Survival

Ron Arias

NAL BOOKS

NEW AMERICAN LIBRARY

A DIVISION OF PENGUIN BOOKS USA INC., NEW YORK
PUBLISHED IN CANADA BY
PENGUIN BOOKS CANADA LIMITED, MARKHAM, ONTARIO

Published simultaneously in Canada by
Penguin Books Canada Limited

 NAL BOOKS TRADEMARK REG. U.S. PAT. OFF. AND FOREIGN COUNTRIES
REGISTERED TRADEMARK—MARCA REGISTRADA
HECHO EN DRESDEN, TN, U.S.A.

SIGNET, SIGNET CLASSIC, MENTOR, ONYX, PLUME, MERIDIAN
and NAL BOOKS are published *in the United States* by
New American Library, a division of Penguin Books USA Inc.,
1633 Broadway, New York, New York 10019,
in Canada by Penguin Books Canada Limited,
2801 John Street, Markham, Ontario L3R 1B4

Library of Congress Cataloging-in-Publication Data

Arias, Ron, 1941-
    Five against the sea : a true story of courage and survival / Ron
Arias.
        p.   cm.
    ISBN 0-453-00703-1 : $18.95
    1. Survival (after airplane accidents, shipwrecks, etc.)
I. Title.
G530.S874A75   1989
910.4'5—dc20
                                        89-35187
                                        CIP

Designed by Sherry Brown

First Printing, October, 1989

1   2   3   4   5   6   7   8   9

PRINTED IN THE UNITED STATES OF AMERICA

**For Joan and Michael,
survivors too**

Acknowledgments

For a book that started as a magazine assignment, I want to thank *People* magazine, my employer, for asking me to report and write the Costa Rican sea-survival story. I especially want to thank my colleagues John Saar, Scot Haller, Jane Sugden, Peter Castro, and Meg Grant for their assistance during the early going. Managing editor Jim Gaines also let me off the hook for six months to research and write the book.

Second, I would like to thank the five fishermen and their families for putting up with weeks of my endless, niggling questions about their lives before and during the nearly five months of the *Cairo*'s fateful trip. In general, the warm hospitality of the Costa Rican people—in particular, the national airlines LACSA—made my visit a pleasant one.

I must also applaud the meticulous efforts of my friend Akihide Teraoka of Fujieda City, Japan, for interviewing a number of Japanese men who were key characters in the story of the five Costa Ricans.

Most of all, I owe boundless appreciation to my wife, Joan, who steered me right in shaping the early chapters, and my son, Michael, who proofread the manuscript and caught some choice goofs.

Last, a word of thanks to my agent, Reid Boates, and my NAL editor, Michaela Hamilton, for helping me take this project through to the end; to Jim Damalas and Rick Squire of Directions International, owners of the film and book rights to the fishermen's story, for asking me to write it; and to Peter Serling and Curt Gunther for providing me with photos of the men and their families.

Contents

Contents

La esperanza es la última que se pierde.

Hope is the last thing you lose.
—Costa Rican saying

PREVIEW

Winds with gusts of up to 120 kilometers per hour continued to sweep most of the country yesterday. Much greater winds are expected today, with no significant changes in the weather foreseen during the next two days.

—Weather forecast in *La Nación*,
San José, Costa Rica
Thursday, January 28, 1988

The man was a gruff-talking Costa Rican fisherman. He was saying he'd been caught at sea a long time ago in something almost as bad as this year's big wind. He was describing how he was pulling in a catch when the north wind had rolled like thunder across the open water. It slapped him down onto the deck and washed over him with a sharp blast of sea spray. Then the boat rose into the air, tilted to one side, and the man and the rest of the crew held on for their lives.

Gradually the waves grew higher and higher, until they towered over the boat. Water poured into the little cabin, and nothing could be seen through the windows. The old-timer was saying he tried to start the engine, but it wouldn't turn over; and the batteries were dead and the radio wouldn't work.

1

They were soaked and sinking, so they did what they could to stay afloat, but they were being pushed farther and farther away from the coast.

He was saying he remembers the wind and the waves smashing open the cabin and sending them all sprawling on the cabin deck. He was stunned and terrified, and he was spitting saltwater and crawling around on his hands and knees.

"Now," the old fisherman was saying, "you take these men on the *Cairo* everybody's talking about. They were caught in something worse. A lot worse. That's why no one's heard from them. You understand me? Not a word. No remains. No bodies. No boat. Nothing. They're gone, they'll never come back."

1] DEPARTURES

Puntarenas, Costa Rica
January 19, 1988

Just before dawn Edith González was awakened by a rooster's crowing. It was a reassuring sound, she thought, an announcement that the world was still here and that the day could now begin. She listened for other signs— barking dogs, birds, a distant cough, muffled voices. A faint light shone around the edges of the window curtains, and she pictured the sky's creamy reddish glow over the mountains to the east. Soon the fishing barrio called Veinte de Noviembre would be filled with the sounds of wide-awake life: babies crying, vendors shouting, boat engines sputtering. But for now, for these few moments by the side of her husband, the time was quiet, peaceful.

Joel González moved restlessly under the sheets. "What time is it?" he whispered.

"Sleep," Edith said. "You don't have to get up yet." For days they had been anxious about the fishing trip planned for today. The last two eight-day trips out into the Gulf of Nicoya and beyond into the Pacific Ocean had been failures, with such small catches that the *Cairo III*'s captain and his four crewmen hardly had any earnings to divide up. Now Joel, one of the crew, was about to leave for another eight days, giving Edith the last of their savings—about fifteen dollars—to buy food for her and their four girls. If the trip went well, he had told her, maybe it would be one of his last. After all, he only worked at fishing out of need; what he really would like to do while he was still young—not even thirty yet—is run a business of his own or work in an office. At least something where he could use his high-school education.

Edith looked at the quiet figure beside her and silently prayed that their luck would change. Joel, she was convinced, was meant for cleaner, less risky work, something with a future. If only he could earn enough to quit fishing, if only the little bakery they had started behind the house with hired help could prosper, if only they could move to higher ground where there were fewer mosquitoes. . . . Suddenly Elke stirred in her crib, and Edith, her twenty-five-year-old body still slender and shapely after four births, slipped out of bed to nurse the baby.

A neighbor:

I don't know what his friends call him, but we called him the Salvadoran. I think he left El Salvador when he was little, but once he'd moved in here, if you asked for Joel Omar González, people would say, "Oh, the Salvadoran." You see, we're all known as something around here. We're getting a lot of Nicaraguans lately, so they're known as Nicas. And of course we Costa Ricans are the Ticos. Then you get all kinds of nicknames, like the Toad or Ugly or Crazy. But really, it doesn't matter where you come from or what you look like. What matters is who you are. Names are something extra.

6:30 A.M.:

Pastor López, another of the four crewmen, hurriedly drank the last of the coffee his wife, Rita, had prepared, then lit a cigarette. After drawing deeply on the filterless tip, he fixed a blank, frowning stare on his sleepy-eyed, four-year-old son, Alvaro; the boy had just entered the tiny kitchen, having left his asthmatic baby brother asleep behind the partition where the family slept.

"The boat's leaking," Pastor said flatly. Rita, who was mixing some cooked rice and black beans together in a saucepan, stabbed the fork into the mound of speckled mush and eyed her husband intently. Pastor then continued in a monotone, "Too much water, too much water, all night too much water . . ."

A small young man with light-brown hair, Pastor was a clam-digger, and it was only in the last month that he had started fishing regularly for a living. But fishing was only temporary, a job he took during the Christmas holidays when some of the boat's regular crew were missing and the owner needed a fifth hand to complete the usual complement of five on board. Today's departure would be Pastor's third time out on the *Cairo III* and the start of his last trip—definitely his last, he had decided. Even though he liked the others on the boat well enough to continue with them, he was eager to return to digging in the soft mud around the mangrove trees. Clamming didn't earn him much, but at least he was his own master. And for a restless, feisty man with a quick temper, a life without many rules suited him fine. "I'm me and I do what I want," he would say with a laugh. "No one bosses me, no one crosses me."

As his son approached for a good-bye hug, Pastor went on about the boat, as if in a trance, saying the leaks in the hull needed patching. Shipworms had eaten finger-size holes in the wood along the sides and near the bow, but worse were the cracks in the higher, sun-exposed planks near the stern. Yesterday they had loaded the water, food, fuel, bait, and ice to store the fish. Now the boat sat lower in the water, which had begun to seep and spurt through parts of the dry, split seams. As the crew's newest member, Pastor was asked to spend the night on board guarding the boat's cargo of necessities, and it was then that he had noticed the water collecting beneath the engine compartment.

"Daddy," Alvaro blurted, interrupting his father's thoughts.

Pastor reached out to hold his son by the shoulders, then knelt on one knee. "Listen, little man," he said, "I want you to do something for me."

"Don't go," the boy said, shaking his head.

"I have to," Pastor said. "Just one more time, then it's back to the clams, I promise."

"And some money," Rita added. "The baby's sick, and if I need more money for medicine, what, then?"

"Look, little Alvaro," Pastor continued, ignoring the question, "just do one thing for me. Pray to God that this trip goes well. Pray with all your heart. Can you do that for me?"

The boy nodded, and Pastor—dressed in short pants and a T-shirt—kissed his wife and son, retrieved a handbag with a few changes of clothes, and left with a smile and a wave.

Hilda Rojas, Pastor's mother:

What got him into prison was a fight in a bar. With a policeman, of all people. Well, what happened in the end, so not to go into details he knows better than I do—what happened was that he was sent to a year and a half on San Lucas Island. That's where he grew up, he said. He learned a lot. That was his classroom, the place where he learned to survive.

Late morning:

Gerardo Obregón, the dark, stocky captain of the *Cairo III*, startled his wife Lidia when he appeared in the doorway of their small, rented house, a cigarette in one hand. "What happened?" she said. "I thought you'd be out to sea by now."

"We're fixing some leaks," Gerardo answered, entering and sitting down at the table with a sigh. "Can you make me some lunch?"

Lidia wiped her hands on her apron, then snapped her fingers. "Lunch. Just like that, huh? Why didn't you let me know you were coming back? I could have bought something. This is lunch for the kids and—"

"Never mind. I'll have coffee."

"Oh, no, you'll eat. I'll fry you an egg with a little rice."

Gerardo, squinting through his cigarette smoke, made a face as if he were gagging.

"Ah, the delicate one," Lidia said. "The lion doesn't like egg, doesn't eat bread. He only eats steak."

It was true. For most of his thirty-three years Gerardo had been a picky eater and a lover of beef. Although he fished for a living, he never liked to eat fish, preferring barnyard meats like pork, chicken, goat, lamb, and his breakfast favorite, beef sirloin, medium rare. The barrel-chested captain had even taken to calling himself a "carnivore," as if he had finally discovered a word whose sound and meaning fit him perfectly. On a wall next to the kitchen table hung a cloth print of a lion, Gerardo's birth sign and spiritual mascot.

Lidia slid a scrambled egg from the skillet onto a plate. Not only did he sometimes blame her for his drinking, she felt like saying, but he would probably blame her for starving him. "Here," she said, plunking the egg and a big scoop of mushy rice in front of him, "you're worse than the kids."

Reluctantly, Gerardo lifted a fork and dug in.

Lidia:

When I first met Gerardo he was living by himself on the boat. He would sleep there and also guard the boat for the owner. All I knew was that he was another fisherman and that he liked to wear dark glasses. He wasn't from around here, so I didn't know him. He'd cook on the boat and even wash his clothes there. I remember on our first date he surprised me by wearing all new clothes—black corduroy trousers and a white shirt. I think he bought them just to look good for the dance we went to. By the time we left, I told a friend that I was going to catch this guy in my own net.

I had lived with another man before and had two sons, but it didn't work out. Now this Gerardo, him I liked. He was a hard worker and he liked me and the boys. So I thought, Why not? Maybe I'll be luckier this time.

After we got to know each other, he asked me to live with him. He gave me money for a place to rent, and one month later I was pregnant. That was Charlene, who's two. With those big eyelashes, she looks just like him.

You know, the day we got together, three years ago, that was the day he was promoted to captain. I guess I gave him good luck. Sometimes he drinks a lot and we argue, but where am I going to get another man who would take a woman like me with kids?

Back then I was working at the tuna and sardine cannery. I started that at fifteen, cutting heads and tails. Then they made me a group captain because I was quick and knew what to do. Seven to ten I would work. Later I left the cannery, then went back when I was separated and needed to work. My mother took care of the kids, and this time I made it to supervisor. I had fifty women and six men under me. When I met Gerardo I had been supervisor for eight months.

I quit because he asked me to. He wanted me to stay

home and take care of the kids and also be around when he got back from his trips. That was fine because he usually made enough money to get us by. The only problem was he would end up drinking a lot of it away.

I never like it much when he's gone because you never know how the trip is going to turn out or what's going to happen to them out there. I always wish him luck when he leaves, and I always expect him back in eight or nine days, never more. Once he stayed out twelve days and I just told him, really angry, "Look, Gerardo, don't ever do that to me again. I worry. I start thinking of what could have happened. No, don't ever do that again."

By early afternoon, the moist air had warmed under a nearly cloudless sky. This time of the year, at ten degrees latitude north of the equator, was relatively rainless, and the crew of the *Cairo III* hoped for clear, calm weather in the days ahead. They were at last ready to cast off lines and motor down the canal to the estuary that led to open sea. They were hours behind their planned departure time; they had hastily plugged the leaks with hammered-in pieces of hemp and were now anxious to get started before something else delayed them. Besides the leaks, there was also yesterday's grocery error. The crew's order of eight days' worth of such staples as beans, rice, meat, coffee, fruits, and vegetables was delivered from the grocer with certain items missing—oranges, onions, and pork cuts. The oversight was rare because local grocers were usually quite careful in filling orders of fishermen about to leave for a week or so at sea. In the case of the *Cairo*'s shortened order, the inexperienced clerk, who was the grocer's son, simply made a mistake.

Gerardo tinkered with the engine's erratic water-cooling system, while Joel checked the old two-way radio. Its

weak signal at sea had often failed them, but it was
something they lived with. Like most poor fishermen
they relied on their experience and wits rather than on
modern navigational equipment. At any rate, few owners
could afford to have luxuries like radar scopes and satellite-
location devices; those were meant for the much bigger
tuna-and-shrimp trawlers that supplied the local canneries. Without weather charts or marine maps, the *Cairo
III* was only equipped with a compass, a depth-finder,
one torn life jacket, a broken flare pistol, and five flare
cartridges.

The *Cairo* itself was typical of most small fishing craft
working the offshore shelf and bays of Central America's
Pacific coast. A squat, tubby vessel, 29½ feet long, it
was built of various tropical hardwoods, sturdily nailed
and screwed together in three months by a self-taught
craftsman and four helpers. Inside the low-ceilinged, eight-
by-nine-foot cabin, six bunks were tiered three-apiece
against two walls. There was a tiny galley with a sink, gas
burners, and a food chest against a third wall, and up
front a wood-handled wheel was set before the front
windows. A small door and window were on each side,
and a third door opened onto the rear deck. Here, under
a sturdy, plywood awning, the men stored their fish catch
in a belowdeck icebox. Inside the cabin, a twelve-inch,
black-and-white TV was mounted on a wall, and, like the
lights, ran off the boat's two, twelve-volt batteries. Under the cabin floor, in the lowest part of the boat, a
thirty-horsepower, three-cylinder diesel engine powered
the three-ton vessel.

Rigoberto Ovárez, builder of the Cairo III:
   Just in bronze screws alone I used about four or five
hundred. And about eight kilos of nails. On the keel I
used about two hundred screws, all galvanized iron. Take

the cabin, for example. I fixed it to the deck with some screws that are six feet long and a half-inch thick. All tight and solid, then I banged in nails everywhere. Solid all around, a solid little boat. No one will tell you otherwise.

Besides Gerardo, Pastor, and Joel, two others were on board for the trip, Juan Bolívar, at forty-seven the oldest, and twenty-six-year-old Jorge Hernández, the youngest. Juan, the cook, was an elfinlike Puntarenas father of six whose thick eyebrows and seemingly perpetual frown helped create his reputation as someone who brings on bad luck. Though he began fishing thirty years ago, when most boats were still sail-driven, he hoped to cut down his fishing and find work closer to home so he could see more of his children, especially his teenage son, Santos, a local soccer star.

By contrast, Jorge was a tall, fair-skinned bachelor who had an air of eager innocence about him, and was the only crewman from the country's interior. He had recently arrived from the banana-rich plains on the other side of Costa Rica and had promised his father this would be his last trip before he returned home to help out on the family farm.

Now, as Gerardo kept the boat sidled up to the muddy bank of the canal, the owner called from the dock, "Seems all right, no?"

"So far, yeah," Gerardo shouted from inside the cabin. He stood with his hands gripping the thick, wooden wheel spokes, intent on leaving while the tide was still in and the water deep enough in the estuary shallows.

The owner, a worried-looking, heavyset man who was also sending off his other boat—the slightly larger *Cairo V*—waved encouragement with both arms. "Baby it for now, and when you get back, we'll take it out for a complete check—leaks, engine, everything."

"Sure, that's it," Pastor muttered from under the rear-deck awning, "baby it, boys, but say your prayers first." Nearby, coiling a line, Juan glared at his wisecracking crewmate. Then Pastor clapped him lightly on the shoulder, saying, "Just a joke, old man. Don't worry."

As the boat moved out into the canal, Joel waved good-bye from the bow to Edith and the girls, who were on the small concrete dock behind their house. The three girls, even the baby, were dressed in white; Lila, Joel's two-year-old Doberman, was beside them, barking and wagging her stumpy tail.

Edith was smiling, thinking about her husband's earlier farewell from the house. He had kissed the girls, patted the dog, then turned to go. "Hey, what's this?" she said. "Them, yes . . . and me? What about me?" Joel, his dreamy, heavy-lidded eyes rolling back for a moment, returned with a grin to kiss his wife. "What are you so worried about?" he said. "You'd think I was going as far as Panama."

"Well," Edith answered, "you never know." Watching him leave, she uttered a simple prayer for him to have a good catch so he would make lots of money.

As the two boats chugged away, children swimming in the canal scrambled for the banks, which were lined with metal-roofed shacks and houses on stilts. Neighbors signaled farewells, and Pastor blew a kiss to Rita, who was standing near the water with Alvaro. The boy was shaking his head, still asking his father not to go, when suddenly a cloud passed overhead, for an instant darkening the *Cairo III*. Feeling strange, Rita grabbed her son and for a long while pressed him to her side. Minutes later, the boats rounded a bend and disappeared into the estuary's main channel.

Late afternoon:

Gerardo throttled down the engine as soon as the voice of the *Cairo V*'s captain came over the radio. The other boat's engine, recently overhauled, was leaking oil and overheating. Could Gerardo tow them back to the owner's dock? Both vessels, with the *Cairo III* far in the lead, had only begun to head out of the Gulf of Nicoya to try their luck along the southern coast. Now Gerardo had to return, already having lost half a day without yet dropping a hook or net into the water; towing in a boat meant more lost hours and they wouldn't be able to start work until close to midnight.

Disappointed, he spun the wheel around and steered the boat back through the calm waters toward the *Cairo V*. Seated on the low, wooden barrier that bordered the rear deck, Pastor joked that maybe the delays were a good way of working out all the possible problems that might occur to them. "Get them over now, right?" Pastor said.

"Go back to clams," Juan replied. "You don't know what you're talking about."

"Excuse me, Your Ancientness," Pastor said, "I was only making an observation."

Jorge, quiet and normally a spectator when the two short men sparred, decided to participate. "Maybe Juan knows something we don't know," Jorge offered.

"I'm listening," Pastor said, eyebrows raised.

Juan gazed into the darkness toward the Pacific. "All I'm saying is that out here anything can happen."

"Brilliant," Pastor said. "And all I said is that maybe the worst is behind us. From now on, we'll catch a few fish. How about it, Grandpa?"

"Whatever you say."

Later, as the smaller boat slowly lugged its disabled sister toward the distant lights of Puntarenas, Joel and Gerardo stood in the cabin by the wheel while the other three were outside. Joel mentioned Juan's remark about more setbacks. Neither man had worked with Juan for very long, but they were aware that some fishermen thought his presence guaranteed poor catches.

"They say he's bad luck—puts a bad eye on things," Gerardo remarked. "What do you think?"

"That's stupid," Joel replied. "You might as well believe in witches and fortune-tellers."

Gerardo nodded, then glanced back to see Juan enter and mumble something about preparing dinner. "Well, he's a good cook," Gerardo said, lowering his voice. Then, shouting over the engine noise, he asked Juan for some coffee.

Juan, eager to be busy and away from Pastor's teasing, smiled and set to work.

By midnight, although the air had turned cool, the shadowy figures on the *Cairo III* were still wearing the usual work clothes of fishermen in the tropics—short pants and a T-shirt, or no shirt. Barefoot under the dim bulbs of the cabin and the rear-deck awning, they shouted farewells to the other crew and pushed away from the owner's dock. They had just shed the weight of the other boat, and Gerardo wanted to leave immediately.

"We're going," he told the owner. "The longer we stay here, the more the ice will melt."

"You'll do all right. You've got, what?—about another six days of ice left."

"More or less."

"So good luck, and God be with you."

Time, Gerardo knew, was just as important in the profit equation as how many pounds of fish they caught. The catch could be stored in chipped ice for about eight days before the ice melted and spoilage set in. So it was up to the captain to bring the boat in on time. The fish—mostly tuna, shark, dorado, snapper, swordfish, and sailfish—was then bought by middlemen who sold it for canning or trucked it to the capital, San José, for export.

Maneuvering the boat into the darkened estuary, Gerardo steered toward a dozen or so yachts moored along the main channel. Next to this cluster of high-masted shapes were several resort hotels, and Joel, seated on the roof, glimpsed a giant, color TV screen hanging in a waterside restaurant. Above the diners, a mini-skirted woman danced to a pulsing rock beat. Joel had never been in the hotel, but he imagined it was a place where the service was first-class, where people dressed well and spoke well. The owners of the sleek sailboats and gleaming cabin cruisers were probably gringos or people from San José. Someday maybe he and Edith could have dinner in such a restaurant, just the two of them, without the girls. For one evening, they would dine like elegant people, without worries about money, unbothered under the big screen.

As the *Cairo III* churned by the string of houses, boats, canneries, and dockside bars, the crew watched the city's glow with a mixture of hazy fascination and relief that the lights were about to be left behind. After passing the gloomy, block-long central market, the boat came within a hundred yards of the coast-guard station, its several high-speed patrol cruisers visible next to the base wharf. And toward the point where the estuary meets the sea, the hulk of the gulf ferry was tethered next to its landing. Above the groan of their own engine, they heard a bus laboring into second gear. But as the unmuffled exhaust sound faded, the rhythmic pulse of a Colombian *cumbia* gradually emerged from somewhere among the midnight dwellers of Puntarenas. For a while the music grew louder, then softer, until finally the throbbing beat faded completely. Later, in the dark after the boat left the city lights behind, Pastor climbed into his bunk and began to sing the same *cumbia.*

"Hey," someone whispered, "shut up."

January 20:

About midmorning, an hour after the crew had dropped their anchor and baited lines for their first day of fishing, Gerardo spotted another fishing boat about a mile away. Since not much was biting, he called the other vessel— the *Yorleni*—on the radio and asked how they were doing. Immediately, he regretted making the call. They reported they couldn't start their engine, their ice had melted, and they had no more food. Would Gerardo help them? The captain told them to wait, then turned to Joel. "Son of a bitch," he muttered.

The problem was the other boat's electrical system, and the two men discussed their obligation to help. In the past few years since they had known each other, Gerardo had come to respect and at times rely on Joel's opinions because he was by far the most educated of the men and his advice was usually sound. As for the rest of the crew, Gerardo treated them gruffly and almost never asked for their opinion.

Reluctantly the captain ordered the lines and anchor pulled up, then radioed they were on their way. He was hoping the *Cairo*'s batteries could start the other engine; then they could return to fishing without losing more time. But nothing worked.

Six hours later, after towing the hapless *Yorleni* back to port, the *Cairo III* edged next to the dock with a glum-faced crew. In return for the tow, the captain of the other boat replaced the fuel the *Cairo* had used while towing. Gerardo planned to head back out about eight P.M.

For hours, he and his frustrated crew had chewed on their situation, grumbling and cursing their luck. Now, while they were at a dock being refueled, Juan told Pastor he was quitting. "I've had enough of this," Juan said. "Everything's wrong."

The two had stepped off the boat, and when they were out of earshot of the others, Pastor gently told his furrow-browed crewmate, "You can't just quit. That's not correct. Who's going to cook? And who's going to do your fishing?"

"They'll find someone else."

"No, papa, that's not right," Pastor began, speaking in clipped, fast bursts. "We need you. If you quit, we might as well all quit, because it'll probably take another day to get somebody to replace you. So we'd lose another day, another day's ice, and what the hell—then for sure, why should any of us go out? No, no, no, papa. You're the one who's going to save this trip. Just by coming along, right now, you'll save the trip. You'll save all of us."

Juan, who had been absorbing Pastor's rapid-fire talk with one hand raised, as if he wanted him to stop, accepted the younger man's logic. But later, as they watched the city lights again retreat into the darkness, Juan thought he had made a mistake. If he had stayed behind, he could have avoided spending four more days on a boat that seemed to be cursed with troubles. Now, it was too late; he was stuck on a leaky boat with a captain who barked orders as if he were scolding animals. How could you respect a captain like that?

It was almost sunrise by the time the *Cairo III* arrived at the previous day's fishing spot, several miles off the rain-forested headland called Cabo Blanco. It was a favorite area not only for commercial fishermen but also for sport anglers, native and foreign. In fact, the deeper waters of Costa Rica's Pacific side are a sportsman's

Eden for catching yellowfin tuna, dorado, marlin, Spanish mackerel, and snapper.

Now, however, little more than an occasional diving cormorant broke the water's surface. A brisk, cooling wind came up from the north, and the low, rolling swells were flecked with whitecaps. It was Thursday, January 21, two days after their original departure, and Gerardo vowed he would do his damnedest to make up for the lost time. They would not fail, not if he could help it.

El Loco Estupinián, Gerardo's fishing mentor:
I met Gerardo years ago when we were both in our early twenties. He was always a hard worker and learned things well. Always curious, always asking how to do things. Never shirked a chore. He was the kind of guy who gives you peace just knowing he's aboard. You know things will get done, even if he has to do them by himself. He's stubborn that way, but the main thing is that whatever it is, it gets done.

He says I taught him everything he knows about fishing. That might be true, because when I first hired him he had just started fishing. Me, I was born to the work. But not him. He had to learn everything—the net, the boat, the weather, when to fish, how to cut, how to clean. We haven't fished together for a long time, but in those days we were like brothers, up and down the coast, good trips and bad trips, in all kinds of weather, side by side. And I'll tell you something: that man never let me down.

Anyway, one thing I told Gerardo is that he should never count on anyone but himself if he ever got into trouble. You're on your own, I told him. If you're ever at sea and get into serious trouble, whatever you do, don't go crazy. That'll do you in faster than anything.

2] A GREAT CATCH

For three days, until Sunday, January 24, the five men on the *Cairo III* followed a predictable routine: up at four or five in the morning to gather the evening's catch in the net; gut and clean the fish; pack it in ice; wash down the deck; eat; rest; fish awhile with baited hooks and weighted lines; throw out the net before sundown; maybe watch a little television and then go to sleep in their bunks.

At night, with the engine turned off, the boat would drift but never far from its original position, since the two-thousand-foot-long net acted as an anchor when the boat was in deep water. Attached to the bow, the net was weighted at the bottom and hung twenty feet down from buoys made of plastic jugs. Surface fish such as sharks and dorados would tangle themselves in the net, and in the morning the men, working from the stern, hauled aboard their prey.

On this morning, Gerardo communicated by radio for the last time with the boat owner in Puntarenas. He reported they had about a thousand pounds of fish so far, a typical "salad" mixture, mostly mako sharks, dorado, and other, smaller fry.

"At least you'll break even," said the owner.

"It's not great," Gerardo replied, "but it's a start. We'll probably head north for a few days. Be back by

Saturday." The captain explained they had some more ice from the second boat they had towed and would stay out a few more days beyond the usual eight-day period. He then relayed regards from everyone, adding, "See you soon—God willing."

From his spot at the wheel, the captain gazed through the thick plastic windows, pleased that the weather and seas were being cooperative. Light swells and a steady, brisk wind continued under a clear sky, and he wondered where they could head next. They had just finished cleaning up after the morning's harvest, and Juan was already busy preparing steaks for lunch.

"Okay, we're going," Gerardo said, clicking on the ignition and throttling forward.

Behind him in the tiny galley, Juan countered the boat's forward lurch by spreading wide his short, muscular legs.

Not long after they moved farther offshore, away from Cabo Blanco's jungle silhouette, Gerardo eavesdropped on a surprising radio report from the *María Cecilia,* another fishing boat from Puntarenas. The voice said they were returning to port with a catch of six thousand pounds they had pulled up off a promontory called Punta Guiones. Gerardo listened intently to the other captain's jubilant description, meant for another boat, then heard the only cautionary note in the transmission. It was a remark about the wind being "a little strange . . . a bit weird." After listening to the conversation, Gerardo changed the *Cairo*'s direction to a northwesterly course, pointing the bow toward the area off Punta Guiones.

They arrived shortly before sunset at a spot about twelve miles from the coast. Stopped in the water with the engine idling, the *Cairo* bobbed placidly in white-tipped swells, while from the north, gusts occasionally whipped sheets of spray over the side, soaking anyone who was outside on deck. Without wasting time, Joel, Jorge, and Pastor set to work throwing out the net, which had been gathered and folded that morning on the cabin roof. Careful to avoid snagging the net in the propeller, Gerardo slowly moved the boat to stretch out the line of buoys in a giant curve. By the time the net was completely paid out, all they could see in the darkness was the blinking, battery-run light at the line's farthest end warning other boats of the net's location.

Gerardo shut off the engine and joined the others for dinner. Pastor turned on the TV set, adjusted the reception, and after changing stations, settled on a movie about the rise and fall of Idi Amin. Filled with action, the story engrossed them all. Pastor was especially excited, replaying images of African faces and places long after he climbed into his bunk, wrapped himself in a thin blanket, and dozed off to the rocking motion of the boat.

About four-thirty A.M., after about six hours of sleep, Gerardo swung out of his bunk onto the floor. Pressing one hand against the ceiling to keep his balance, he nudged Juan, who slept below him, and Joel, who was curled up in the top bunk. The captain then turned on the cabin light and poked the other crewmen, Pastor and Jorge. The swells had grown since the night before, lifting and dropping the boat so there were moments when the crew seemed suspended off their mattresses. With a few groggy moans, one by one, they all left the cabin to step out on the rear deck. There, clutching an awning post for balance, the five voided their bladders over the side.

Before long, Juan heated the coffee and handed out steamy cups with bread, bowls of scrambled eggs, fried sausages, and beans. Stomachs filled, everyone except Juan, who was busy cleaning up the galley, began to haul in the net. Normally a job for three men, it took four to fight the pull on the net exerted by a heavier, wilder sea.

At sunrise, though they already had worked an hour, they felt as if they had only begun. While keeping their balance on the tossing deck, they tugged sections of the net over the side, untangled the fish, clubbed the ones that were still thrashing about, and piled them to one side. It was tiring, tedious work because they spent much of their energy trying to stay upright. Yet it was soon obvious this was no ordinary catch. Mostly dorados and four-to-six-foot sharks, they spilled over the deck in piles, some still twitching, until the men hardly had space to work or store the net.

"We saved ourselves on this one," Gerardo remarked gleefully at one point. "It's cash from here on." Pastor slapped his hands together, rubbing them back and forth as if he were about to eat; Jorge broke into a big grin; and Joel said, "I'm already counting."

About eight o'clock, after they pulled up the net, they spent the rest of the morning gutting and packing. They tossed the entrails overboard, then cut off and discarded the unusable heads and tails of the sharks. Later, while the other men cut and rinsed the meat with seawater, Gerardo hunkered belowdeck in the icebox to receive the fish. He stacked them in the chipped ice that already filled the hold. The larger sharks were halved and Gerardo packed enough ice around to keep it all uniformly chilled. The icebox itself, which was insulated and measured about four-by-five-feet square and three feet deep, was then capped by a heavy, unhinged cover that fit down snuggly over the slightly raised, square opening of the hold.

Gerardo, the one responsible for the crew's success or failure, was especially careful to properly store and cover their cargo of potential earnings. He had packed away perhaps twelve hundred pounds of meat, so with what they already had, their total rose to about twenty-five hundred pounds—or a lot more than most eight-day trips produced. That meant about $900 for the boat's owner, $300 for him, and $150 for each of the crew. One or two more lucky days like today would double these amounts and they would return home heroes. The men laughed and already seemed to be celebrating.

Gerardo, sorry he had argued with Lidia before leaving, thought of buying her a necklace or giving her the down-payment money for the sewing machine she wanted. Or maybe they could get married. Yes, make it official, a big wedding, a big party—anything was possible when you had the money.

It was noon by the time the men finished washing the deck and themselves of blood and bits of fish flesh. Exhausted and hungry, they escaped the wind and crowded into the cabin to feast on Juan's concoction of potatoes, rice, beans, and chicken.

"Hey, Juan," Pastor called from his corner spot where he squatted on the floor, "you're improving. This isn't so bad."

Juan, a fastidious organizer in the galley, cursed the ship's heaving, which made the water he was boiling for coffee slop out of the pot and douse the flame coming from the gas burner. "Keeps putting it out," he muttered, holding the pot within the guard rail that circled the burner.

"Here," Joel said, tossing the cook a white throwaway lighter. "Test it, it's new."

Juan caught the plastic Bic with one hand and snapped down on the tiny wheel at the top with his thumb. "Thanks," he said, and lit the burner after several tries. Tossing it back to Joel, he asked, "What are you doing with a lighter? You don't smoke."

"I don't know . . . Somebody gave it to me. I must've thrown it in my bag by accident."

"Maestro," Pastor shouted, banging a spoon against his bowl. "What's for dessert? Bring on the dessert."

Using a long chopping knife, Juan sliced open a ripe papaya, cut the yellow inside in long, slender pieces, and handed a few to Pastor.

Gerardo, seated on the floor by his bunk, congratulated everyone on their good luck. Normally quiet, with a serious expression, the curly-haired captain with the thick black mustache smiled and said in his deep, gravelly voice, "Finally, we hit the lottery. It's a great catch."

"A toast," Pastor said with a grin. He clinked his metal cup against Jorge's nearby elbow. "To the beautiful sea, thank you for your gifts!"

Mouths full, the others smiled and signaled with a raised arm or cup. Even Juan shifted his attention a moment from his chopping block and sink to turn around and nod.

Later, they spent several hours throwing out lines, each with a number of baited hooks to see if they could snare more dorados or sharks. By four in the afternoon, they had caught two or three of each. Gerardo, boosting himself up on the side rail to look over the cabin roof, watched the foamy tips of the swells. Far away, maybe fifteen miles, he could see a dark line of hills.

The boat hadn't drifted too far during the night. If they threw out the net for one more night, they would still be close enough to the coast to find shelter. It wouldn't be the first time he had to run for safety when fishing. The trick was knowing when and knowing how reliable the engine was—especially the engine, because without power, you might as well be a piece of driftwood.

Earlier in the day, Joel tried the two-way radio and discovered it would only receive and not transmit. Now, when Gerardo turned it on, only intermittent static came from the speaker. He was hoping to pick up a report on the wind, which he and the crew were calling a *norte*. Never a certainty, the *norte* was a rainless scourge from the north that only struck in the early months of the year, hitting gale-force velocities that could whip the seas to thirty- and forty-foot heights.

Gerardo was wondering what the weather reports predicted, wishing he still had the old AM radio they had left behind—when Pastor shouted from outside. He and Jorge had seen two of the large Puntarenas tuna trawlers about a mile and a half away. "It looks like they're heading back," Pastor said. Curious, Juan, then Gerardo, emerged to have a look. Gerardo studied the boats for a while; they appeared to be heading parallel to the coast. "No," he said, "your eyesight is bad. They're staying out."

"I don't think so," Pastor said excitedly. "It looks like they're running for the coast."

Frowning deeply, eyebrows touching, Juan added, "Gerardo, are you sure? Seems to me they're going right to the coast."

Gerardo answered, shaking his head in a definite no.

Jorge, a head taller than Juan, glanced up from his worried crewmate and also tried to gauge the direction of the two trawlers. After a moment, he shrugged, undecided. The supporting cross beams of the awning were only about six feet above the deck, and the five men, gripping the beams above them and facing inward along the four sides, looked like human table legs in discussion. The swells seemed to increase in height, but the wind was about the same, blowing spray over the bow and stern deck.

"Maybe they're right," Jorge finally blurted. "I mean the wind *is* hitting pretty hard. They're probably getting out of this."

Pastor turned around to see if he could glimpse the

high-prowed trawler when a blast of spray caught him in the face. "Look, Gerardo," he said, wiping his face with one hand, "I don't have your experience. I've never been fishing in a *norte*. But this one looks like it's about to blow hard. What do you say we head for shore?"

With the engine shut off, the boat rode the dark-blue swells with the ease of a fat seabird resting on the water. At the top of a rise, Gerardo clearly saw the distant line of coast. "We've been out in worse than this," he said casually. "Isn't that right, Joel?"

Without hesitating, Joel answered, "Yeah, sure, we've seen worse."

"Well, I haven't," Juan shouted, "and I was out here fishing before you two were born."

Gerardo glowered at the smaller figure and asked, "Are you afraid, or what?"

"I'm not afraid. But I know when I'm right. You just can't stand it when one of us is right."

"And you're crazy wrong. Maybe you do bring bad luck."

Interrupting, Pastor looked at Gerardo and said, "Listen to him. What's crazy is what you're doing."

Joel gestured for Juan and Pastor to stop arguing. "It's getting late, and this is getting us nowhere."

"What is it with you, Joel?" Pastor asked. "You run the boat or what?"

"Okay, that's it," Gerardo snapped. "This is no place for sissies. Let's go! Throw out the net! We'll just stay this one night and leave in the morning."

After Gerardo ducked in the cabin to take the wheel, Juan and Pastor continued grumbling. Suddenly Juan, who was distracted with this talk, caught his thumb in a tangled part of the net that was being let out in the water. Screaming in pain, he tried to wrench it free, while the others pulled on the net to prevent it from pulling him overboard.

At that moment Gerardo appeared, saw what had happened, and began shouting for Juan to yank his hand out. When he finally did, moaning and cursing his luck, Gerardo told him to quit bellyaching and get to work.

Glaring at the captain, Juan said, "Animal! You think I'm an animal. Well, *you're* the animal!"

"Listen, old man," Gerardo said flatly. "Don't be lazy. You get to work. And if you're no use here, stick to cooking." Gerardo glanced at the injured thumb, muttered his annoyance at the delay, and returned to the wheel and throttle, to turn the boat to keep the line from snagging on the propeller.

"Son of a bitch," Juan continued outside, cradling his thumb. Jorge, Joel, and Pastor, still struggling at the stern, uttered sympathetic remarks about the mishap. If the crew lost a man to an accident, it would only mean more work for the others.

Before long, as the four men relayed sections of the net to drop overboard, they decided it was worth the risk to stay another night. One more catch like this morning's and they'd be rich men—well, practically. Just one more great catch would do it.

Shortly after sunset, Juan went in to prepare dinner, and the others finished dropping the last of the net over the side. The light buoy blinked in the distance, and the stars were filling the darkness above. Before following the others, Pastor, without a word to anyone, took a coil of unused rope kept on the cabin roof, then looped and knotted it around the four awning posts at waist height. Pastor yanked on the makeshift guard rail, which was probably strong enough to hold the weight of three men. Fishing boats did not have rope rails around their stern decks, but then they were seldom caught out at sea by a *norte.* The vision of himself falling into such a whipped-up ocean terrified him. Give me a river or an estuary, he thought, wishing he were back in his flat-bottom skiff, paddling out for clams. But not this, not these waves, not this blackness, not this constant heaving up and down, up and down. "Listen to me, Lord," Pastor said, leaving his handiwork. "Keep me on this boat. Please."

Inside, the five settled on the floor or in their bunks to eat their portions of food. Juan announced that the meal wasn't elaborate because he kept burning himself by trying to keep things from tipping over. One of the crew wisecracked that the older man had wide feet and spread-out toes "like a monkey's," perfect for a cook's job. They all laughed, even Juan. His short stature and splayed feet allowed him to move on deck with a surer, more agile step than the others, which helped when working with hot foods and utensils in a narrow space.

After dinner, Gerardo ran the electric bilge pump for awhile. He had run it on and off throughout the day, guessing that either the hull seams had not been sufficiently caulked or the water on deck was running into the boat's lowest section—the engine compartment in the center hold. It could even be the wood-eating shipworms, marine insects usually kept off hulls by toxic paints; the *Cairo*'s bottom paint had long ago worn away. But the flooding below didn't worry him too much, since pumping had kept the water level from rising. And, besides, they would return to port soon.

Just before eight, they turned off the overhead bulb, leaving on the red-and-green warning lights outside, and climbed into their bunks. With one good catch behind them and the prospect of another only hours away, anticipation and excitement increased in the dark. Alone with their thoughts and random comments, Jorge and Juan already imagined themselves back home with money to spare; Joel said a prayer for a good catch; Gerardo was listening to the incessant thumping noise the net line made yanking itself taut every time the boat pitched up, and Pastor chuckled to himself, remembering Dumbo in the cartoon movie he had seen earlier on the TV set: the little elephant who flew was his kind of hero.

By eight o'clock the boat began to roll to one side, then right itself and roll again. Tied at the bow to the long, heavy net, so far the *Cairo III* had faced the wind and oncoming swells with its flat stern; now, with the waves suddenly higher, perhaps by ten feet or more, the boat was slapped broadside by the breakers at the top of the swells. To avoid being thrown, the men pushed against the berth or ceiling above them with one hand, and gripped the side rail with the other. There was nothing else they could do except listen to the louder bashing of waves against the hull and cabin, the ominous creaking of beams and planks, and the more insistent thunking of the net line. They were tired and sleepy, but no one could sleep, thinking this was a *norte* and these were the biggest waves any of them had ever known. Water now swept over the cabin and leaked through cracks in the roof.

"It's ugly, really ugly," Joel kept repeating.

"Start praying," Pastor urged.

Jorge muttered something about the rain on the Caribbean side of Costa Rica and how it would hit from the north and go on for days.

"But it's not raining here," Pastor said.

"I'll tell you what," Juan interrupted. "We wouldn't be in this mess if we hadn't thrown out the net."

"Don't play dumb," Joel said. "You wanted more fish just like the rest of us."

Gerardo vaguely caught their voices; he was concentrating on distinguishing the other sounds of the boat's battle with the waves. Were they louder or sharper? Was that a new sound? Was something breaking or ripping? He envisioned the roof peeling away or the windows breaking. Occasionally he interrupted his imaginings, left his bunk, and stumbled across the wet floor to operate the pump switch near the wheel. It had to be monitored. If the bilge water ran to one side, leaving the pump intake exposed to the air, it would have to be primed with water to start working again.

"But if we hadn't stayed—" Juan continued.

"Goddamn it, old man," Joel cut in, "that's the risk you take. Are we kids or what?"

"Listen, Juan," Pastor said, "when we come out of this, we'll be dancing all the way to the bank. But first, God wants to put us through a little test. Later, we can count our—"

The boat tilted steeply to one side. Jorge lost his grip, tumbled out of his bunk, and landed on the floor next to Pastor's berth. Pulling himself up, Jorge poked Pastor. "Let's just get through the night."

Around midnight, a sudden, strange calm enveloped the boat. One moment the men were fitfully trying to sleep and at the same time hold on; the next moment they seemed to be lifted from their slender, sponge mattresses, raised in the air, then gently lowered, again and again. They still heard the wind and the creaking of the boat, but the swells and breaking waves appeared to have abruptly abated. "Thank God, it's calmed down," Joel said. In minutes everyone had fallen asleep.

Sometime after four A.M., Gerardo swung his legs over the side of his second-tier bunk and dropped to the floor. Groping in the dark, he reached the rear door and opened it. Outside, he held on to the awning and peed into the wind. The swells seemed to have grown, but he couldn't be sure because the movement of the boat was smoother.

Perhaps it really had calmed down. Now if only the wind would die down . . . Then they could pull up the net, store the catch, and leave for home.

Gerardo listened for the thumping noises made by the thick net line yanking against the bow. Hearing no such sounds, he reached up and, gripping the roof hand rail, scooted along the outside of the cabin to the bow. He then crouched on the narrow deck and felt for the net line that should have been tied to a stout, square post in the middle. The line was gone.

Returning to the cabin, Gerardo switched on the ceiling light bulb and roused the crew. Amid some grumbling and half-awake stares, he told them, "The net broke."

"What?" Joel cried, sitting up.

"It broke, ripped right off."

Unbelieving, the four crewmen scrambled from their bunks and ducked outside into the blasts of wind and spray to check for themselves.

"No," shrieked Juan.

"Ay, papa," Pastor cried, squinting into the dark.

"Maybe we can find it," Jorge suggested. "Maybe it's right around here."

"Forget it," Pastor said. "It happened hours ago. That's why everything got calm. *El norte* fooled us . . . and we thought it was easing up."

Disheartened and angry, the four crewmen returned to the cabin to face the captain.

Gerardo had turned on the engine and the outside spotlight, which was fixed to the front part of the roof. "We'll look for it," he told them, spinning the wheel to head the boat into the waves. "And if we don't find it, we'll run for the coast."

Juan glared at the burly figure working the wheel, thinking the man should have listened to them. But

Gerardo was stubborn, always giving orders, always playing some kind of macho role. Juan shook his head, trading anxious glances with the others.

Finally Pastor, trying to stay upright, told Gerardo it was his fault they had lost the net. Joel then said it was the captain's right to give orders and—if it happens— even to make mistakes.

"Well, he sure made a big one this time," Pastor said.

"You don't think he knows it?"

"We told him," Pastor said. He was about to light a cigarette and continue when Gerardo shouted for them to grab hold of something—they were about to be hit by a huge wave.

Without looking out the window, Jorge and Pastor dropped to the floor, Juan clambered into his bunk, and Gerardo and Joel braced themselves next to the helm. Just before the impact, the boat dipped its bow and everything turned dark. Above, the eastern sky was just turning crimson with the coming dawn.

It was Tuesday, January 26.

3] *EL NORTE*

On Wednesday *el norte* struck the Puntarenas area at full force, ripping away sheets of metal roofing, tearing limbs from trees, and smashing windows. It was "like the tail end of a hurricane," Gerardo's wife, Lidia, said later. "Coconuts and mangoes were being knocked out of trees, planks of wood were flying through the air. If you were outside, you could hardly stand up."

Gerardo had promised her he would never stay out more than eight days; it was already the ninth day. Looking at the trees bending in the wind, Lidia turned from the window and told her mother she was going outside. Could she please watch the kids for a while? "Maybe the *Cairo*'s been seen," she said, moving quickly toward the door. "Maybe they're coming up the canal at this very instant."

"So, go," her mother said, "but be careful. Watch out for the mangoes."

Lidia gripped the door handle, closed her eyes, and pushed the door open enough so she could slip out. It banged shut behind her and she started across the street, shielding herself from the giant swirls of dust and debris sweeping over the rutted, dirt road. As she hurried toward the street that led to the canal, she passed in front of Joel's and Edith's house and glimpsed an open curtain in the front window.

As far as Lidia knew, Edith socialized with few people outside her family; the two fishermen's wives met only occasionally and that was in the street or at the little all-purpose, neighborhood store. If their husbands were not working together, they probably would have little reason to greet each other at all, unlikely ever to be friends; their backgrounds and interests were so different. Both were mothers in their mid-twenties, but Lidia came from a poorer family and had worked full-time since she was fifteen; Edith, whose origins were practically middle-class, had had a more sheltered upbringing. Edith lived in a big house of her own, Lidia in a small rental. And Edith's husband, Joel, was a frugal, private person, a cautious drinker who liked sports and shunned parties; Gerardo was a generous, sociable beer-drinker who would rather party or tend to his vegetable garden than play soccer or any other sport.

Now, as Lidia passed Edith's two-story, rose-colored house, she heard a horn blast from one of the returning boats. Skipping over a fallen branch, she leaned into the wind and began to run.

That morning Edith was watching her three older girls finish their breakfast of milk, bread, and scrambled eggs. Edith herself had barely eaten since yesterday when the winds had grown stronger. As she coaxed her next-to-youngest, Tracy, to finish drinking her milk, Edith listened to the tree branches whipping against the roof, the windows rattling in their frames, all the odd creaks, bangs, and whistlings assaulting the house. "My God," she whispered, "when is he coming?"

The girls paused and stared at their mother. Normally Edith was cheerful when the girls' father was about to come home from one of his fishing trips. Whenever she heard that the boat had arrived and the men were unloading the fish, she would hurry to get the girls ready in starched, frilly dresses, ribbons, white shoes, and white socks. In the backyard, Lila would be barking and running around, and they would all rush out to the canal to wait for Joel on the dock. Sharon, Tracy, Emily, even the baby, Elke—all would be waving and smiling, the same as when he left. But today the girls noticed their mother was frowning, as if her stomach hurt. She kept squeezing her hands together and walking around the room, whispering things.

Edith cleaned up after breakfast, nursed the baby, then asked a friend to watch the kids while she went out to ask about the *Cairo III*. She stood on the small concrete dock behind the house and began asking the crews and captains of returning boats if they had seen it, if they had heard them on the radio, if they knew where Gerardo and his men were. No one had seen or heard from them. Every time a boat appeared from the estuary, Edith's hopes rose. But she always recognized some feature—the color of the trim, the cabin shape, the number of windows—something so she knew it wasn't Joel's boat. She waited for it to come close, then shouted her questions. Some of the boats—and there were all kinds, from uncovered *pangas* with outboard motors to bulky thirty-five-footers with cabins and big engines—tied up nearby, and she raced over to ask more questions. Were they sure they had not seen the *Cairo*? Where could they have gone? What was the wind like? What were the conditions?

Having just battled their way back to port, the men blurted terrifying descriptions of big waves, swamped decks, and cabins littered with falling objects. Hearing this, Edith backed away, silent, watching the men join their families, embracing and kissing their wives. Why them and not me? Edith thought. She was sorry she had asked God for money, sorry she had not simply asked for his safe return. A good catch no longer mattered. Forget the prayer—she would never again pray for money. What was important were lives, the lives of the men, the life of her man—that's all that mattered.

While Edith and Lidia stalked the banks of the canal and the nearby streets for news of their men, Pastor's wife, Rita, and her two boys huddled from the windstorm in the family's two-room shack, a rental made of odd-sized, wooden boards roofed over by scraps of corrugated metal. Expecting the roof to fly off at any moment, Rita was afraid it would also rain and then they would be in a worse mess. She wanted Pastor to cover all the holes and patch over and paint the walls. He should have returned yesterday, the end of the usual eight days. But Carlos Rohmán, the *Cairo*'s owner, told Rita they'd be back Saturday. He talked with them by radio last Sunday, and that's what Gerardo said—Saturday at the latest. But in this wind, Rita figured, maybe they would come back sooner, maybe today or tomorrow.

She lit a cigarette, inhaled deeply, and remembered how little Alvaro begged his father not to leave. Before, when Pastor went clamming, Alvaro would clap his hands and say, "Papi, dig, Papi, dig." Her body trembled and she moved to hold her sons close. The two had been wrestling on their bed, and now as they sat one on each side of her, they heard something hit the roof and roll off. "Papi come?" Alvaro asked, peeking up at his mother.

"Yes, Papi come."

Pastor's neighbor:

What do I know? I watched him grow since he was a little boy. I know he's got a mother, and Hilda's a good mother. But maybe he saw me as a second mother, I don't know. Whatever it was, he was friendly from the start. I don't care what his troubles have been, and I hear about them; to me it doesn't matter because he's always been good to me. Respectful. Funny. Always with some little joke, some compliment, even for an old lady like me. And of all the kids around here, and I've seen dozens grow up, Pastor is one of the sharpest. Definitely one of the sharpest—I mean quick. The man can't stay still. He's got to be active. Ask anyone who knows him. He's got to be doing something.

On Thursday Edith's desperation grew as she realized almost all the boats from the canal area except Joel's had returned. The fishermen she spoke to tried to console her by saying the men of the *Cairo III* probably took refuge along the coast and would head for port as soon as the wind let up. And maybe the boat's radio wasn't working so they had no way to report their situation. "They're smart guys," one old-timer told her, "they won't do anything stupid. Besides, whatever anybody does, God decides it anyway. So why get all excited?"

Edith fought the images of the *Cairo* tossing about in the ocean, of the boat breaking into pieces, of Joel struggling in the water. But no, she thought, these were only her fears speaking. The boat was anchored in a safe place along the coast; the men were just waiting for *el norte* to pass. Carlos Rohmán said the boat would be back Saturday. Gerardo had told him so on the radio. But she remembered that was before the wind came up. Wouldn't they return sooner, like the others?

With the wind at her back, her housedress billowing before her, Edith was pushed into a run along the dirt passage leading from the canal to the paved road where the bus stopped. Except for a skinny, short-haired dog trotting across her path, the dusty street was deserted. An empty hammock swung between a lemon tree and the veranda of a small house; fishing nets flapped against fences and walls, and a lopsided, wooden gate squeaked open and shut, open and shut.

To reach the bus stop, Edith crossed a seldom-used airstrip that bordered one side of the fishermen's barrio. She passed through a break in the fence, followed a worn path through an uneven carpet of dry weeds and grass, then raced across the asphalt strip past an old, single-wing crop-duster parked next to a small hangar. Leaving the airstrip, she hurried alongside the high white wall of a cemetery. As she passed the entrance, she quickly made the sign of the cross over her face and chest, then continued to the main road and the bus stop.

On the ten-minute ride into downtown Puntarenas, Edith sat on the oceanview side of the bus. Gazing at the endless expanse of white-capped waves, she again began to imagine Joel at sea, then turned her head away to look at the estuary and mangrove trees on the other side. This stretch of road, this narrow entrance to the peninsula on which the city was built, was unprotected by trees or houses, and the wind blasted one side of the bus with a sudden, whistling fury.

Swooping frigate birds, their scissorlike tails spread wide, dropped low over the first buildings and larger houses that soon rose on each side of the asphalt strip leading into Puntarenas proper. Since it was the start of the dry season, there had been a rise in the city's tourist population—people mostly attracted by the peninsula's long beach, the coast's usually relaxed, vacation atmosphere, sport fishing, and the boat trips out to a string of nearby islands with plenty of protected wildlife, idyllic coves, and palm-shaded picnic spots. Today the tourists and just about everyone else stayed indoors.

By the time she was on the sidewalk near the central market, Edith thought only of saving Joel. She reached the coast-guard station two blocks away in a near panic, breathlessly telling the uniformed man at the entrance that she wanted to speak to the station commander. While he went off with her request, she peered in at the clean, shiny-cement surface of the floor, at the high, warehouse ceiling, at the gray machinery, at the small boat to one side, and out the opposite end through the giant, open doors, at a large, gray patrol boat. Edith looked beyond a group of men in sailor denims gathered around a table talking and laughing, and she wished she could order them to help her. They could find the *Cairo* with their patrol boat. What else was it for, if not for rescuing people in trouble? Right now it was just sitting in the water, tied up to the station, doing nothing.

"Please," the guard said, returning, "follow me."

Moments later Edith sat down before the on-duty commander, a genial, mustached man who asked her how he could help her.

Trying to speak calmly and clearly, she explained her worry about the *Cairo* not yet returning. Would the coast guard search for the men? All the other boats have returned, but the *Cairo* hasn't. Obviously something has happened to them.

The commander replied that the coast guard—actually the naval branch of the Public Security Ministry—would of course initiate a search-and-rescue operation. But first the *Cairo*'s owner would himself have to report the boat's loss; he, not a crew member's wife, would have to appear in person at the station. For the time being, the commander said, she would have to wait and hope that the men had taken refuge along the coast. He added that for several days, warnings of the wind and sea conditions had been broadcast by the coast guard on emergency frequencies.

Captain Stanley Garrón:

Sometimes they ask for the impossible. We try to help but really, our patrol boats aren't made to be towing boats. Our boats are made for high speeds, not for towing. It's hard on the engines, ruins them. But you tell that to these fishermen. You know what they do? This is what they do. They call us for help on the radio. They say their engine's out or the batteries don't work or they ran out of fuel. So, okay, something's got them stranded.

Then what do they do? They tell us their location is somewhere off the north coast, maybe three hours out. Just somewhere. That's all. Three hours out. No latitude, no longitude, no speeds, nothing but the compass direction. Now tell me, how are we supposed to find them? Do you know how immense an area we're talking about?

And of course no one else knows where they are because when they find a good fishing area, they don't like to let the other boats know where they are. Or they'll throw them off by giving a false idea of where they are.

No, it's impossible sometimes. It's like the needle in the haystack. You have to be a magician to find these guys. But we try. Just look at the dispatch log. We're out there a lot. And, yes, we do find a lot of them and bring them back in. We send out a plane, they're spotted, then one of our boats goes after them. But just the diesel we use going out to get them costs more than some of their boats are worth.

And most of these guys aren't even equipped to go out. Not really. They aren't trained in ocean navigation and survival, they don't use charts and maps, they can't tell us where they are. No life jackets, no binoculars, no flares. And so on. It's sad and I know they're poor, but it makes our work difficult. What are we supposed to do when they tell us they're three or four hours somewhere

off Cabo Blanco? What was their speed? How fast was
the current? How much have they drifted? Can we get a
satellite fix of the location? Of course not. Needles in
haystacks don't have that kind of equipment. So we take
a guess and look. But it's only a guess, nothing more.

On Friday, January 29, *el norte* continued blowing as
strong as on the previous two days, and by the time Lidia
visited Edith for the first time, both knew that the last
fishing boat had returned without news of the *Cairo*.
Edith had told Carlos Rohmán that the coast guard
needed him to show up in person to report the boat
missing. But the owner wanted to wait till Saturday to
see if the men returned as Gerardo said they would.

"That's absurd," Lidia said, the two women seated on
a sofa at Edith's house. "How many more days have to
go by with the wind like this? No, sir! The man has to go
down there and sign that report."

Edith tilted her head to one side and was staring blankly
at the floor. "I was just thinking," she said in a wistful
tone. "Before they left, Joel came back for lunch. I
didn't expect him. He was so hungry he couldn't wait for
me to prepare the beans and rice. So I fixed him two
eggs. He started eating right away, but then he heard the
boat start up. 'Sweetheart,' he said, 'the boat's going.'
And then he said he was going to let it go and that he'd
catch it in town where the boat has to pass by. It was as if
he didn't really want to go. But he did. He changed his
mind and left right away. Didn't even finish his eggs."

Lidia waited a moment, then added, "At least he likes
eggs. Gerardo—well, sometimes I think he doesn't like
anything but steak. Before he left we ended up fighting
over a stupid egg or something. My God, the whole thing
was so stupid."

"Lidia, something's happened to them."

"What?"

"Yes, I can feel it, in my heart I can feel it. Hasn't that ever happened to you—when you just know something for certain?"

"Like what?" Lidia said. "What are you saying?"

Edith glanced back toward the rear of the house where the girls were playing. "I don't know what it is exactly, but something happened. I can't explain it, I just feel it."

"Well, all I know is that Gerardo's never later than eight days. Never. I don't care what he told Carlos Rohmán. I know what he promised me. He's not coming back Saturday . . . he just won't."

"So let's go see Carlos," Edith announced, rising abruptly.

"Wait," Lidia said. "What about the other wives? Maybe they should go with us."

Edith didn't know Pastor's wife, Rita; Juan used to have a wife but they had been separated for years. As for the tall one, Jorge, he was still single.

"All right," Lidia said, "then it's the two of us."

A while later they crossed the narrow metal footbridge that arched over the canal at a spot about a half-mile up from Edith's house. The canal itself, about fifty feet wide and two miles long, was built to give barges access to a fertilizer plant at the far end. In one direction, the plant smokestack loomed in the distance; in the other direction, on both sides of the canal, TV antennas, rooftops, and telephone poles rose amid waves of heaving green tree branches.

At the bottom of the bridge, they turned left and hurried along a path parallel to the canal until they came to Carlos Rohmán's two-story stucco house. One of the larger houses in the neighborhood, it backed up on the canal so that he could moor his two boats to a tree or to his small wooden dock. Edith and Lidia looked in the back, saw no one, then knocked on the front door. His wife answered and led them to her husband.

A heavy man in his early forties, Don Carlos was seated in a rocker in one corner of the tile-floor living room. He excused himself for not rising to greet them right away; he wasn't feeling well lately. The women vaguely knew he was a diabetic and had other internal problems. Desperate and ignoring his condition, they pleaded for him to contact the coast guard.

"Let's wait till tomorrow," Don Carlos replied. "They said Saturday, so let's see."

"But what difference does one day make?" Edith said. "What if they're in trouble?"

"I promise, if they're not back tomorrow, I'll go to the coast guard."

"Please," Lidia said, "we think something's happened to them."

"Don Carlos," Edith added, "the coast-guard planes and boats are just waiting there. All you have to do is make a report in person."

He was adamant about waiting till the next day. He also wouldn't budge from his rocker that day.

So the two women left and walked back across the canal. Tomorrow, without fail, they would not leave until he kept his promise.

On Saturday the winds eased, and the local AM radio station reported the coastal waves were decreasing. By late afternoon the air had grown still and it was apparent to the women that their vigil by the canal was hopeless. This time when they approached Carlos Rohmán, Pastor's young wife, Rita, was with them, distraught as the other two.

"We're not just asking you to make that report," Edith said, tears dropping onto her lap, "we're demanding you go."

"All right, all right," Don Carlos answered. "But it's too late."

"What?" Lidia shrieked.

"The office closes till Monday. I'll try tomorrow, but that's all I can do."

"I don't believe this," Edith said in a choking voice. "All we do is wait and nothing happens."

"I'm sorry," Don Carlos said with a pained expression. "I really am."

The next morning, Sunday, January 31, the Puntarenas coast-guard station recorded the report of a local fishing boat that had not returned to port and was presumed missing at sea. Coast-guard officials assured the boat's owner and the crewmen's wives that after receiving approval from higher authority in San José, they would carry out the usual search-and-rescue operation called for in such cases.

A description of the *Cairo III* and a request for sighting information would be broadcast every two to four hours on emergency frequencies, in the hope that other vessels or planes might spot the missing boat. Consulates of neighboring countries would be notified in case the boat appeared on their coasts. And several planes and at least one patrol boat would carry out search-and-rescue sweeps of the area in which the boat was last reported. In the words of its owner, as stated in the coast-guard report, the *Cairo III* was "somewhere toward the north with an unknown destination."

4] THE BIG HOLE

The giant wave hit the boat broadside, and Joel got up off the floor sputtering to the others that the net was the last thing they should worry about. "Forget it! Let's just find the coast and save our lives."

Gerardo, who was still gripping the wheel, agreed they shouldn't waste fuel looking for something that was probably miles away from them. From now on, reaching the coast was their only goal. "Now bail," he shouted, and the others scrambled to find a pail or bowl or pot to scoop up the water that sloshed around their ankles.

The waves had risen to enormous heights, heaving the boat up from the bottom of one trough, then slamming it down the steep slope of the next. Gerardo peered through the foamy spray exploding up over the bow, trying to discern a pattern. But they seemed to come from both sides, sometimes singly, sometimes in quick pairs. Working the throttle with one hand and steering with the other, he kept the bow plunging head-on into the next oncoming wave. The engine propeller and short stubby rudder were useless when the boat tottered on the wave's crest, so he decelerated, scouting for the best angle to attack the next wave. Then he accelerated as the *Cairo* raced down the slope, sometimes straight to the bottom, sometimes diagonally or on a zigzag course. Above all, he avoided being hit broadside again. If they capsized in such seas, even a miracle couldn't save them.

Gerardo could see ahead through three small square windows, and to the sides through the windows of both doors in the cabin's forward section. The thick plexiglass windows were set in wooden frames, with the front three securely latched on the inside. As long as the windows and doors remained shut, the water running in from roof leaks and from around doors and windows could be controlled. So far, the electric bilge pump took care of most of the water flooding in. But several times when Gerardo let the engine idle, the boat rode more smoothly with the waves instead of into them, allowing the others to bail water through an open door or window.

From early morning, when the giant waves began, till after one P.M., Gerardo remained on his feet at the wheel, struggling to keep a thirty-degree, north-by-northeast heading. It was, he believed, the most direct course for reaching the coast. Since he had always fished within sight of land, he didn't need charts or maps or anything more than good eyes and a compass to navigate. But this time, even when the boat rose on the highest crests, the captain saw nothing but an endless swash of waves beneath a light-blue sky.

Before wearily giving up the wheel to Joel, Gerardo looked at the time on his wristwatch, then cursed his inability to gain sight of land. Seven hours of throttling forward, idling, forward again, playing the waves, up and down, muscles straining, nerves taut, waiting for the big tilt, the deafening blast of some rogue breaker he hadn't seen—seven hours of this, and nothing! Had they made progress? Was the north wind that struck them straight on now pushing them backward and farther out, away from the coast? And the current, which way was it running? Where was the coast? How far? Had he at least kept them in place so that when the wind died, they could run right in? They still had plenty of diesel left, but if this went on much longer, the fuel would go, and then what?

"I did what I could," Gerardo told Joel in a tired voice. "Just keep it at thirty degrees." With a nod and a muttered "Take over," he pushed away from the wheel and for a while braced himself by Joel's side. By tacit agreement, Joel was the next in line to pilot the boat, the only crew member Gerardo trusted at the helm. Juan and Pastor were too short to see very well out the front windows, and Jorge had hardly ever steered a boat at sea. You'd have to tie those three to the wheel just to keep them standing. They prop themselves straight up, don't bend, and don't know how to spread themselves. Then they get knocked off their feet. No, it's better if they bail or stay in their bunks.

Pastor:
That first day without the net was horrible, bad all around. What can I say about it? Well, on that day Joel and Gerardo were the only ones at the wheel, spelling each other, just the two of them all day long. They didn't want to give us the wheel, not to any of us. They decided they were the most able, maybe because they had spent the most time on the boat, who knows. . . . The thing is that they felt they were the most capable. I mentioned it to Jorge and I told him, "I feel sorry for these guys, what they're doing to themselves. They should put one of us at the wheel, at least for a few hours, for a little while. But if they figure they know what they're doing, well, then let them do it."

While the others worked the pump, bailed, or clung to their bunks, Joel wrestled with the wheel most of the afternoon. Since he was a teenager driving his father's fish delivery truck in El Salvador, Joel liked maneuvering any vehicle, taking curves, accelerating, calculating speeds and times, staying alert, efficient, feeling the machine. Now, at the *Cairo*'s helm, nothing responded; the lumbering, waddling craft obeyed only the giant, upswelling push and pull of the waves. But though the boat was slow and awkward, it still required constant attention. Some new challenge, some massive shadow on the right or left, some wall of froth rising ahead, something new always faced him. The intense focus on steering and working the accelerator soon let him "feel" the vessel as he once did his father's truck. Every breaking wave, every spray-filled gust, every noise of the engine, every crashing, wood-creaking sound of the hull and cabin—all absorbed him. He moved on instinct, responding only to the moment, to the instant that might avert disaster.

Behind Joel, Juan was crawling across the cabin floor like a spider. "Very little left," he mumbled after looking into the food dispensary, a larder with not much more than some sugar, salt, coffee, and a few handfuls of rice. "If you guys want, I can try to get out some of our shark and dorado. I can make a stew."

"That's okay, forget it," Pastor said from his bunk. "Anyway, it's going bad. I got this whiff of rotting fish."

Jorge swept the puddled water off the vinyl surface of his mattress. "I smelled it too," he said. "You wouldn't get me near that stuff. Not to eat."

"But, damn it, I'm hungry," Pastor cried. "One meal a day, what's that?"

"Sorry," Juan said, "but from now on you won't even have that."

"Will you guys shut up for awhile?" Joel shouted, his gaze never leaving the windows.

"Yeah, all right," Pastor said. "Concentrate."

Gerardo, dozing in his second-tier bunk, tightened his grip on the bunk's side board. It was about five in the afternoon, the sun was low on the western horizon, someone had just turned on the cabin light, and Joel was trying to see clearly through the blurred, plastic panes. Suddenly a mountainous shadow rose ahead and slightly to the side. Just as Joel started to spin the wheel to head into the mountain, the sky darkened and the boat descended into the trough.

The water hit them hard, bashing in the front windows and a door, knocking Joel off his feet and flooding the engine compartment and cabin. While the men clung monkeylike to anything they could grasp, the boat turned on its side, half its hull exposed to the air, then slumped back to right itself. With the inside swamped, the engine stopped and everyone in knee-high water frantically searching for something to bail with, the *Cairo* was starting to sink. It floated heavily, lower than before, and the smallest wave easily washed over the sides and deck.

Amid frenzied curses and shouts to hurry, the men bailed for their lives. They tossed the water out the rear door, a side window, and into the galley sink. No one stopped. Adrenaline-fueled, they stooped and scooped and flung the seawater out at a maddening pace.

"That's it! That's it! . . . Move, move! . . . Give me that bowl! . . . Hurry! Faster! . . . Son of a bitch, it's sinking! . . . Shut up! . . . Move over, give me room! . . . Do it! Do it! Bail, goddamn it, bail!"

At one point Gerardo tossed aside his bowl and stepped outside to retrieve several gallon-sized plastic jugs they used as buoys; he cut off the bottoms and, gripping the handles of each jug, scooped with both hands. He and Joel hammered two-inch nails into the frames of the side doors and front windows to keep them firmly shut and the water from pouring in. Slowly they made progress.

Less than a half an hour after the monster wave smacked them, they had pumped and bailed enough so they no longer would sink. In the dim glow of the cabin light, the glistening, nearly naked figures moved quickly and mechanically; soon the water stopped slopping from side to side and over the lower bunks.

Then a second massive wave hit them with as much violence as the first. The doors and windows popped their nails and water cascaded into the cabin, terrifying the men, who floundered about for a grip to regain their footing. Again, they almost capsized, and again they bailed for their lives. For three hours the five struggled in a race against the sea. Either they won now or they lost everything. If two enormous waves could hit and swamp them, what could three, four, or five such waves do, one after another? Hour after hour, ignoring fatigue, they bailed with a furious intensity. It's what had to be done; nobody stopped bending, lifting, and emptying.

About eight P.M., Gerardo called a halt. "Rest," he said, explaining he would throw over the anchor. The water was far too deep for the anchor to reach the bottom, but the heavy, dragging weight might slow their drift. For a long while no one spoke as they stretched out in their bunks. Then Pastor whispered a thank-you to God and a plea for continued good luck.

"If that's good luck," murmured Juan in an exhausted voice, "what's normal luck?"

Joel made a disgusted sound with his lips and said, "Always with the negative. Just shut up."

"It's true," Juan said. "What's going to happen the next time? We could die."

"Just be ready."

"To die?"

"No, dummy, to bail."

"Quiet, you guys," Pastor said.

Jorge, curled under a moist blanket, had briefly thought
of drowning right after the waves hit, but then the constant bailing demanded all his attention. Now the notion
of death surfaced in his mind as he listened to his
crewmates' voices, to the creaking wood of the boat, and
to the breaking of each wave against the cabin side.
Gerardo had nailed the doors and windows shut, but
would they hold? Jorge pictured his father alone at home
in Río Frío, on the other side of Costa Rica, and wondered if the wind had struck their farm? Was there rain?
Would his father need him? My God, he thought, what
have I done? I could have stayed and gone home and I
didn't. He wanted me home. And look what I did, look
at this. Papa, what's going to happen here? What's going
to happen?

Early Wednesday morning, January 27, as soon as he
could see enough to maneuver, Gerardo started the engine and gave the order to bring up the anchor. All night
the anchor line had made a loud banging noise against
the bow. Next time he would throw out an old tire they
had on board. Maybe this kind of anchor would be
quieter.

Outside, conditions were about the same, the wind and
waves continuing to pummel the boat. Inside, under the
cabin floor, the water was halfway up the sides of the
engine compartment and about to slosh into the cabin
itself. It was an awkward, confining space to bail from,
so they took off deck planks above the engine to make
bailing easier. Soon the level was enough for the pump to
control most of the flooding.

During the night, Gerardo thought he heard a ship's
engine. It seemed faraway, but if one passed by again,
night or day, they should be ready with a signal—maybe
the spotlight, or a flare, maybe some smoke or fire,

maybe a radio call. In the morning he told Joel, and Joel, for years an electronics tinkerer, set to work trying to repair the radio. After removing the casing, he dried the larger parts, replaced the casing, checked the power from the batteries, then tried in vain to transmit a call for help. The radio was dead.

Joel had more success with the flare gun. He replaced a broken plastic part near the firing pin with a scavenged piece of metal, and the pistol was complete. But he wouldn't know for sure if it worked until he fired one of their five cartridges.

For a while during the morning, Pastor took the wheel. As Joel and Gerardo had done, he fought to keep the compass on a thirty-degree heading. At first he imagined the boat moving closer to shore, but that was difficult because he could see no land, and soon it was all he could do to make it to the top of the next wave. It seemed as if the *Cairo* careened up and down on the wild rails of a giant roller coaster. The boat would labor up to the crest, hesitate for an instant on the peak, dip its bow, then zoom down over the surface, plunging down and down, toward "that big hole in the water," as he told the others, "that hole that wants to swallow us as if we were nothing."

Once, after he took his place at the helm, Pastor was convinced the big hole was about to swallow the boat. As he was racing toward the bottom and the boat began to plane sideways, into the curl of the big wave, the windows burst open with a tremendous rush of water. One of the doors wrenched itself free of the nails, slapped him hard in the face, and slammed him to the floor.

"Hey," someone screamed at him. "Lazy! Get back up and steer."

"Up, man, up," another added. "You can do it. Let's go, Muscles!"

Stunned, spitting water, Pastor scrambled to his feet and again attacked the wheel while his amused crewmates started bailing and Gerardo fetched the hammer from a toolbox. Later, after closing the door and windows, the captain took over the helm.

By now the smell of rotting fish in the icebox was oppressive. Almost as one, they decided to dump the shark pieces overboard. For more stability and so they wouldn't have to fight against the waves, Gerardo stopped the engine and all but Juan ducked out the rear door. Outside, under the awning, they gathered around the open icebox hatch, and with one hand clutching Pastor's makeshift, guard-rail rope, they began to toss the hunks of shark over the side. A small amount of ice remained at the bottom and this they packed around the arm-size dorado.

"Here, it's cheap," Jorge yelled to no one in particular. "It's free! Eat your rotten, stinking shark!"

"What the hell, it's just money," Pastor added, turning his head away from the stench.

"And Juan?" Gerardo asked. "Where's Juan?"

"Asleep," Joel said. "I don't know, he's lazy or something."

"Juan!" Gerardo called into the cabin.

"What?"

"Let's go, this is your shit too."

"Not mine."

"Get out here."

"It's your mess, not mine."

Gerardo, working steadily, shrugged and remained silent.

Later, as they were clearing out the hold, Pastor mentioned making a sail to push the boat faster toward the coast.

"We could stretch a blanket between the posts," Joel suggested.

"Who knows how to sail?" Jorge asked.

"I know a little," Pastor said. "But His Ancientness in there knows it all."

"Yeah," Joel blurted, "but look at him! You'd never get him out here to help us. What good's an old fart if he's just smelling up the air?"

"Maybe," Pastor said, "but I'll talk to him."

After disposing of the shark pieces, the four on deck began to fillet some of the dorado in the hold. They believed it was less spoiled and that strips of dorado flesh could somehow be dried and eaten later on. They cut off several dozen pounds of the strips and put them on the cabin and awning roofs, hoping the wind and sun would convert the white tender flesh into a kind of jerky. They all complained of hunger and had gone almost two days without eating anything more than watery rice with some squid they had brought along as bait. Yet no one was tempted to sample the dorado.

Wednesday night passed without a major incident to clear the bunks. They threw out the tire sea anchor, cut the engine, switched on the pump every so often, and in the darkness of the damp and tossing cabin they tried to sleep. Again they heard the faraway, pulsing sounds of ship engines. Several times Gerardo and Joel, who both had waterproof watches with luminescent dials, checked the time and even went outside to look for lights. All they could see were the stars and a three-quarter moon. Their work since that first day of fishing off Punta Guiones had drained them of energy. They fingered the dorado strips. The flesh was still mushy, moistened by the continual, windblown sea spray. In the morning, they decided, they would have Juan cook some strips.

By Thursday morning, the twenty-eighth, just after Joel and Gerardo choked down a few boiled pieces of the now-stinking dorado—the others refusing—only eight gallons of diesel remained in the ninety-gallon fuel tank; two days of struggling against the wind and current had used up more than they had expected.

Joel suspected they would soon run low, and approached the captain. "Gerardo," he began, "with the fuel we've got, it'll be impossible to reach land. It's dumb to waste it and leave ourselves with nothing. Why don't we save it in case some ship passes by? We move closer, and they'll see us. What do you think?"

Gerardo liked the idea but Pastor objected. "No, no," he said excitedly. "Let's just go, go as far as we can, until the diesel runs out. If we get there, great. If we don't, well, at least we tried." After listening thoughtfully to both suggestions, Gerardo turned off the engine.

They were now in the coastal shipping lanes that run from Panama to California or northwest across the Pacific to Asia. In the afternoon the wind speed dropped slightly and the biggest waves, instead of rising to four times the height of the boat, decreased to two and three times. They were still hit by the occasional odd wave that smashed open the windows and doors and swamped the cabin, but the worst of the storm was passing.

In the early evening, with the engine cut and the tire anchor overboard, they saw the first ship they had a chance of attracting. They had seen others on the horizon, but this northbound freighter or tanker—they weren't sure—looked as if it might pass within about fifty yards of their boat.

Joel fired two cartridges in quick succession. The burning orange flares rocketed high over the waves in two smoking arcs, then dropped to the water in a sputter. They turned on all the boat's lights and, ignoring the sheets of spray that slapped them, stood under the awning waving their hands and shirts and yelling for help. As the ship slowly neared, the waves burst over the bow in gigantic, thunderous splashes. Then the ship slowed almost to a stop, and a powerful spotlight blinked on to capture the *Cairo* in a blinding glare. Apparently carrying chemicals of some sort, the ship also gave off a nauseating, acrid odor.

Overjoyed, Juan darted into the cabin and began stuffing his belongings into a small suitcase. He was about to fill someone else's bag, happily muttering, "To hell with this boat—let's pack up and go!" when someone outside said the ship was leaving. "No," Juan shouted, emerging from the cabin. The spotlight had been turned off, no one was visible on the ship's deck, and soon all they could see were the retreating lights of the bridge.

"No, no, no," Juan moaned. "But why?"

"Probably thought we were all right," Pastor said. "Lights on, anchor out."

"But we were telling them—" Jorge began.

"They couldn't hear us," Gerardo said. "Nobody was even outside."

"Juan, forget it," Pastor said. "Hey, old man, there'll be others."

All that night, someone stood watch at the helm or outside without sighting another ship.

By ten the next morning, still drifting, everyone except Juan was outside stripping the last of the dorado when Joel spotted two freighters coming toward them in the distance, one on each side, a black-and-white vessel and an orange-colored ship. After a brief, excited discussion, they turned on the engine and ran toward the orange ship. After they started moving, Joel realized the black-and-white ship would pass closer to them first, so he fired off a flare. There was no response; that left them with two remaining flares.

Gerardo now hoped to intercept the route of the orange freighter, and as they came within a hundred yards of the ship, Joel fired another flare in the air. Desperate because no one responded and because the ship would soon leave them behind, Joel fired the last flare. For a few minutes the men frantically waved shirts and blankets, shouting continuously. Although they were sometimes hidden in the wave troughs, on the crests they were plainly visible. Yet no one noticed them.

Angry and profoundly disappointed, they stared after the orange shape until all they could see was a plume of dark smoke on the northern horizon.

"What's the point?" cried Juan, slumping onto the deck, one hand on the guard rail. "All this chasing for nothing."

"Joel, any more flares?" Gerardo asked.

"That's it."

"I'm telling you," Pastor said with a disgusted shake of his head. "We've got to run for land. It's our only chance."

"And use up all our fuel," Joel added.

"What good is it out here? We might as well keep trying for the coast."

"Pastor's right," Juan said. "Unless some guy's outside emptying the garbage on those ships, they'll never see us."

Jorge, who agreed with Pastor and Juan, left to check the diesel tank to see how much fuel was left. While he was gone, Gerardo and Joel returned to cutting strips of dorado.

"What do you say we eat some of this," Gerardo said.

"It's rotten," Juan replied with a disgusted expression. And Pastor believed the putrid meat would make them sick.

"Then you guys are the dummies," Gerardo said, slicing into a dorado. "Haven't you figured it out yet?"

"Figured out what?" Juan asked.

"You eat, you live."

"Yeah," Pastor said, "but put some of that in your mouth and who knows how long you'll live."

"That's not what I mean. I'm talking about staying alive."

"So?"

"This is it. You eat, you live."

"What, are you going to tell us what to eat?"

Jorge appeared with the news that they had about nine gallons of diesel left in the tank.

"So what do we do?" Pastor asked Gerardo. "Run or stay?"

While the boat wobbled and pitched on the heaving sea, the captain gazed at the still-cloudless horizon, in the direction of land, then glanced at the four shirtless, weary figures. After four days without much to eat, the shadows were deepening between their ribs. "We run," Gerardo said.

Juan:

In those first days, when Gerardo wasn't near us, we talked about it a lot. We said that if we could have gotten ourselves out of that situation by killing him, then we would have killed him right at the very beginning. We all had that intention, but we decided we had nothing to gain by killing him. What would that have accomplished? The mistake had been made. Of course, if he had listened to us before the net broke, nothing would have happened. But he didn't. He had to have his way. We told him but he wouldn't listen.

I suppose Pastor and I stirred up things the most. But it wasn't until toward the end that we told him we were ready to kill him. Because of your stupidity, we're here where we are. He never said a word, just kept quiet. We even told Joel that he played a part in this because he didn't back us up at the beginning. We asked him, "Why didn't you support us? If Gerardo had taken our advice, we could have stayed close to shore. We could have followed those two trawlers in. But, no, you wouldn't listen. You went along with him, and then it was too late."

We were angry—me, Pastor, and Jorge. I mean, we were ready to kill Gerardo if it would have saved our lives. But we didn't know for sure what was going to happen. That's the only reason we didn't go through with it.

5] MISSING

When she was a little girl, Edith had longed to be an airline stewardess. Growing up in a place bordered on three sides by water, a narrow, tropical city with one slim exit, she dreamed of escaping to a cooler, less confining world than Puntarenas. To fly in an airplane, to travel about dressed in heels and a smart uniform, seemed like a perfect way to live. Year after year her German father would leave home to work as an electrician on Caribbean cruise ships. Away for months at a time, he would return—sometimes in his handsome white uniform—with presents from other countries and picture postcards of sleek, modern cities. Edith believed they were wondrous, elegant places somehow accessible only by working—possibly as a stewardess.

However, her father discouraged her, and by the time she entered high school, her dream of a career in the air had faded. Instead, she looked forward to a few more years of school, marriage, and several children. Her mother, who ran a popular downtown bar, never allowed Edith to help her at work because of the coarse atmosphere and because the quick-tempered teenager might offend or anger some of the customers with her feisty nature. Marry a man with a profession, her mother counseled, someone who would rise in the world.

But Edith married a pudgy Salvadoran who would

soon drop out of high school in his last year. Although he was a serious, ambitious boy and her sweetheart ever since they met on the city's beach promenade, Joel González could offer her only a meager room in a crowded house he shared with several relatives and family friends in the poor barrio bordering the canal. A house his parents in El Salvador helped buy, the dusty, unfinished structure was far less comfortable than the spacious, tranquil home of her parents. The teenage couple had to face the hardships of supporting themselves and raising the first of four daughters. So Joel dropped out of school before graduation and set to work fishing.

As if to remind her of her fantasy, Joel's house was near the area's only airport, an asphalt strip used occasionally by crop-dusters, coast-guard spotters, and other small planes. The takeoffs and landings of planes were a visual treat for her girls, a curiosity, a sweet memory of a time when anything seemed possible.

After Joel and the others were officially reported missing by the coast guard, Edith passed by the airstrip and prayed for deliverance of a different kind. What she wanted was not for a girlhood dream to come true but for a certain aircraft to arrive. It would appear from over the ocean, swoop down on the city, land and roll to a spot where she and the girls waited. The engines would stop, the door would open and the first face, the first figure to appear would be Joel's.

It was this vision that flashed before her when she heard her mother's voice one morning. "Wake up! The planes are out looking for them!"

Edith almost never slept till midmorning, but ever since she thought Joel was in trouble, she couldn't rest at night and barely managed on a few hours' sleep in the morning.

"Come on, get up," her mother urged. "You don't have to cry anymore."

Edith focused on her mother, an expressive, dark-haired woman who now stayed the nights with her to help with the girls. "You're sure?" Edith said, getting out of bed.

"Go see for yourself."

In minutes Edith was dressed and out the front door. She kept telling herself, Stay calm, control yourself, slow down, walk, walk, don't run.

"Lidia, Lidia—the planes are here," she shouted as she rushed by Obregón's house.

"She's not here," Lidia's mother answered from within. "She's with the planes."

Edith skipped over the road's dry potholes and slick, protruding rocks. Unable to restrain herself, she ran. The houses, yards, faces in windows, people walking in the street or riding bicycles, someone waving a hand, a dog curled and warming in the sun, kids shooting marbles in the dirt—all were distractions, vague hurdles meant to slow her, to keep her from what mattered the most. Her lungs hurt and she felt she would never reach the airstrip, still a half a mile away. Finally, as she turned a corner, she saw the familiar white cement fence posts that surrounded the landing field.

"Wait up," a voice called, and Edith turned to see her best friend, Myrna, just behind her.

"Hurry," Edith cried, "there they are!"

Ahead, across the middle of the strip, were two propeller-driven planes parked on the far side. Three or four men looking at a map stood by one of the planes, a green one, and nearby Lidia waited with a group of neighbors.

Edith tried to remain calm, but overtaken by her emotions, she raced across the asphalt and went right for a tall, mustached man in short pants and a uniform shirt. He held a wrench or pair of pliers in a grease-blackened hand and was laughing about something with the others. To Edith, he looked like the pilot.

"Did you find them?" Edith asked, her eyes wide open and close to tears. "What have you found?"

The tall man smiled at the young woman with the crazed expression. "What are you talking about?"

"The men of the *Cairo III*. Did you find them?"

"Ah, yes. I mean, no. We don't know anything. I don't even know if I'll go up today."

Edith glanced at the map held by one of the men. "Please," she cried, "find them."

"Lady, calm down."

"I'm fine."

"That plane's out, it won't fly," he said, casually nodding to the plane farthest away. Then he chuckled over what seemed a private joke between him and the other men. "And this one here is in bad shape."

Edith closed her eyes, now running with tears, and prayed the pilot would say, "Ma'am, you get right into this plane, and I'll take you up. We'll fly until we find them. We'll do everything in our power to find them. Leave it to us. We'll find your men."

"Can I see the map?" she asked at last.

"I don't know," he said, pausing, toying with the moment. "That depends."

Lidia then approached from behind and put an arm around Edith. "It's no use. The planes are just for show. He did a little turnaround in the gulf, and that was it."

"Lady," the pilot said with a grin, "what we're doing here is just having a look around. We can't go far or we'll run out of fuel. You want us to get lost too? Maybe drown?"

"Please," Edith pleaded, "look for them."

"You're hysterical."

"I am not!"

"Lower your voice."

"I'll speak the way I want."

"Look, I told you, it's too dangerous. Besides, we're probably wasting our time." He threw up his hands with an exasperated expression and began to turn away.

"Wait a minute," Edith said.

"Lady," he muttered, "leave us alone."

"What's your name?" Edith demanded, her face reddening.

But the pilot laughed and stepped away.

"What's your name?" Edith persisted.

He ignored her and began talking and joking with the others.

Later, while walking home, both wives crying, Edith said, "Was it money? Did he want money? My God, I'll find every cent in the—"

"Save your money. What we could give wouldn't buy him cigarettes."

"He *had* to know we were the wives, don't you think?"

"Sure he did. It was all over our faces."

"But he was so nasty."

"Because he doesn't care. You think they care?"

"Lidia, he wasn't even respectful."

"Of course, not. They see us like a piece of nothing. We're nothing."

After a while, still crying, Edith unclenched her fists, unfolded a handkerchief, and blew her nose. "What are they good for?" she said, sniffling. "They don't go any-where. Oh, they're good for taking important people out to an island or someplace. But us? When we have an emergency, forget it, it's not important."

"Too dangerous."

"Maybe run out of fuel."

"Or get lost."

"Drown, he said."

"Edith . . . ?"

"Hmm?"

"I'm afraid. Really afraid."

Coast-guard log:

January 31. Took down a report by a Mr. Carlos Rohmán notifying us that his fishing boat, the *Cairo III*, with a crew of five, is missing at sea. Its last whereabouts, says the owner, was somewhere toward the north with an unknown destination.

February 2. Sent the information concerning the *Cairo III* to the general staff in San José.

At 10:00 hours, began emergency-frequency broadcasts at regular intervals three and four hours apart, giving the information about the *Cairo III* and requesting assistance in locating this boat and its crew.

At 14:20 hours, a search plane departed from Puntarenas to look for the *Cairo III*. About two hours later it returned without having sighted the boat.

Feb. 3. At 7:45 hours, the search plane left for the second time to look for the *Cairo III*. The pilot and navigator were instructed to begin the sweep from our northern territorial limit with Nicaragua and continue south in an arc with a ninety-mile radius out from Cabo Blanco. The plane returned several hours later. The *Cairo III* was not sighted.

News report:

More than two weeks have passed since the *Cairo III* was reported missing, and the search continues. However, coast-guard spokesmen said, "Hopes are fading and we do not discount the possibility that the air and sea sweeps will soon be discontinued."

*   *   *

"Go to San José," Edith's mother had told her. "Get together the relatives of the men and all of you go to San José. That's the only way to get some action. Talk to the coast-guard bosses, talk to ministers. If you have to, talk to the president. But go right away. Don't waste time. You're getting nowhere here. Just making yourself sick. Now go, go, go. Get the others and go."

Edith knew her mother was right. Everyone she talked to was convinced nothing was being done to find the *Cairo*. The patrol boat she saw on her first visit to the station was still tied up, and no one had seen it move for weeks. Even the coast-guard men on duty gave her different answers, some saying they had searched at sea and others reporting the patrol boat had never left its mooring. Apparently, the order to send out the boat was inexplicably delayed in San José.

The three wives—Edith, Lidia, and Rita—were deeply depressed by their inability to do anything. Every day they asked for news at the coast-guard station, at the docks where other fishing boats tied up, or at the home of the *Cairo*'s owner. The answers were never encouraging and almost always darkly negative. They even heard rumors—later discounted—of bodies washed ashore in Panama, bodies of men that could be from the missing boat. One published report had them shipwrecked somewhere off the coast of Colombia. A commercial airliner spotted the men clinging to the wreckage and somehow managed to drop them food and supplies. Later, even after Colombian authorities announced the report was a fabrication, the rumor persisted with local, often grisly embellishments.

Perhaps the person worst affected was Hilda López, Pastor's mother. When someone told her they'd heard on the radio that some of the men were found alive but that her son's gruesome remains—or what the sharks failed to eat—were among the dead, she fainted on the spot. Her daughter-in-law, Rita, immediately had her mother taken to the area's only hospital, where a doctor declared the elderly lady had suffered an attack of nerves and would have to be hospitalized. Such an attack, they said, could cause heart failure.

Because Hilda, normally a lively, combative woman, was ill, Rita couldn't go to San José with Edith and Lidia. Carlos Rohmán, the *Cairo*'s owner, also declined to accompany the women, excusing himself because of his poor health. His brother Jorge Rohmán, also a boat-owner, volunteered to go in his place. Also, two sisters of the *Cairo*'s bachelor and youngest crew member, Jorge Hernández, said they would join the group in the capital, since they were coming from the other side of the country.

For most of the two-and-a-half-hour ride, Edith and Lidia remained silent and somber. The large, comfortable bus jogged up from the tropical lowlands through the cool, coffee-growing mountain valleys, stopping a few times to pick up passengers until the aisle was filled with newcomers. As the bus climbed a steep valley, at certain bends and stretches of the highway the two wives glimpsed the dull gray sheen of the Pacific Ocean far away in the morning's sunlight. Finally the bus hauled itself up the mountainside, leaving behind all view of the sea and their home below. They had made the trip many times before, but never with more sense of purpose.

Among the Central American countries—indeed among all Latin American nations—Costa Rica is unique for a number of reasons. It is a stable, democratic, peaceful enclave located between the conflictive states of Nicaragua and Panama. The size of West Virginia, or 185 miles across at its widest point, it has no standing army—

only a relatively small police force to keep order. Costa
Rica has also set aside 13 percent of its territory—or
proportionately more for its size than any other country
in the world—to be used for national parks, reserves,
and other conservation lands. Because of its five distinct
climate zones, from sub-alpine to tropical rain forest,
these protected areas are spread along both coasts, over
four mountain ranges—including spectacular volcanic
peaks—and the lush valleys of the interior.

The Puntarenas travelers by now had seen at least
three of the climate zones. More than an hour had passed,
and they were climbing through the highest, coolest part
of the coffee-growing mountains, where supposedly the
country's best coffee beans are harvested. The slopes
became steeper and steeper, until near the crest of the
saddleback pass only single rows of the lustrous, dark-
green bushes fit on the neat terraces etched up the side.

After the bus descended into the country's broad, central valley, Edith nudged Lidia. "How're you doing?"

Lidia straightened the lap of her green knitted dress.
"Okay," she said.

"So quiet."

"And you?"

"Same," Edith said, offering a sad, little smile. She
was also wearing a dress and heels and had added a
touch of red to her face. "Lidia, don't you think they're
hungry? I mean, by now they must be out of food, no?"

As if she had been asking herself the same question,
without hesitating Lidia replied, "Gerardo hates fish. I
can't tell you how much. The other night somebody
brought over some turtle meat. I asked him to try it, and
what does he do? He spits it out."

They were silent for a moment, vaguely watching a
citrus orchard, then a field of corn, flit by the window.
"If I eat," Edith said, "I think I'm taking from him. Joel

has nothing and I'm taking what's his."

"I've thought of that, but Gerardo's so picky he wouldn't want most of what I eat. Before he left the last time, he promised me when he came back he was going to change. He said he'd stop drinking so much, that he'd stay home more, that he'd even marry me, all formallike in the church. Poor thing—he promised he'd change in everything but that."

"That?"

"His eating."

"Of course . . . his eating."

"My lion only eats meat."

As of 1988, Costa Rica had a population of more than two and a half million people, mostly descendants of early Spanish explorers and settlers who set to work farming a land of raw, earthy riches rather than plunder an advanced native civilization, as their brethren did elsewhere in the Americas. In fact, it was Christopher Columbus—the first European to arrive in the area in 1502 on his final voyage—who christened the land *costa rica*, rich coast, because of its natural beauty. In the following centuries, the central valleys were mostly divided into small farms whose prosperity depended on coffee exports. In this century bananas, grown on the coastal plains, have become the other major export, along with the recent addition of African coconut palm oil. As for fishing, especially small enterprises like that of the *Cairo III*, this industry forms only a minor part of the export economy.

San José, with more than 600,000 inhabitants, is the controlling hub of Costa Rica. And because of the country's small size and a fairly modern system of highways connecting towns and cities to the capital, there is little sense of isolation in outlying areas. If you want some-

thing done, if you want the government to act on something, you go to the capital. Of course, a bureaucracy
exists, but it is generally very personable. Informality is
the rule, and even presidents and ministers are often
seen chatting with constituents in the streets and outdoor
cafés. Such easygoing access to the ears of power was
probably why Edith and Lidia thought they could actually spur the government to action in the first place.

As the bus rumbled by San José's international airport,
the women could already see the cluster of downtown
buildings glinting in the distance. The four-lane, divided
highway led past commercial centers, luxury hotels, parks,
and finally into a busy, major boulevard that cut through
the heart of the business area. Because the city's eleva-
tion is more than 3,700 feet, the air was cool but comfortable, and most people in the streets wore shirtsleeves
and blouses under light sweaters and jackets. Edith and
Lidia stepped off the bus into the brilliant, midday sunlight, for a moment feeling energized by the dry, cooling
breeze, so different from the clammy dampness they felt
back home. They were also excited by just being in the
big city, joining the sidewalk crowd of animated, well-
dressed people on the move.

Visitors to Costa Rica's Foreign Relations Ministry
seldom enter through the front. The sweep of stairs, the
big doors, and the single guard outside appear to be for
show; most of the daily business is done around at the
sides of the square-block complex of offices. When the
Cairo III group arrived to plead for government action in
their case, an officious clerk in one of the side offices
told them the minister only gave audiences to certain
select people and with many days' prior notice. They
would have to make an appointment. In the meantime,

they could try speaking with another, lower official at the opposite end from the ministry's imposing facade.

They entered the small, rustic, converted house by way of a veranda just off the public sidewalk. Several women were typing and filing papers in a crowded outer office. The visitors asked one of these secretaries if they could speak to Victor Monge and explained why. She disappeared with the request behind a set of narrow double doors with glass panes, returning moments later to show them in.

A handsome, mustached man about forty rose to greet them from behind a large desk in the center of a spartan, slightly musty room. He gestured to the straight-backed chairs that the clerk was now arranging. The visitors sat down and, beginning with the boat owner's brother, stated the situation. Weeks had passed since the men were reported missing, and yet the government had done little to find them. Some radio broadcasts and a few quick flights over the ocean had failed to produce even a clue about the boat's fate. They could be in Nicaraguan, Honduran, Panamanian, even Mexican waters by now. Would it be possible for him, a foreign-relations expert, to help start an international search for the men? Not only their lives were at stake but also the welfare of wives, mothers, and children. Please, could he do something?

Victor Monge listened patiently to the desperate voices, now and then asking a question or commiserating. "Look," he said after they had finished, "look behind you." They turned, expecting to see a person. Monge continued, stepping from around his desk and approaching a wall map of the Pacific Ocean. "Let's see," he said, pointing to Costa Rica, which was smaller than the size of his finger. The visitors gathered around. "If they left from here, they could have caught currents that would take them here, to the north, or here, to the south, toward Colombia." He paused and caught the pained expressions of Edith, Lidia, and Jorge's two sisters.

"And the wind?" Edith asked.

"That would have pushed them out, maybe far, especially if their engine wasn't working."

Lidia began to cry.

"Ah, I have to tell you," Monge said in a warm, direct way. "Some years ago, I forget how many, one of our fishing boats was lost for a few months and turned up near Hawaii."

His guests stared at the finger tracing an arc across from Central America to the Hawaiian Islands.

Returning to his desk, Monge ignored his ringing telephone and assured them he would personally contact all consulates of countries in the region and ask for their cooperation in locating the missing boat. The women were also encouraged to call him anytime, and he promised to help if he could.

"What about the coast-guard patrol boat?" Lidia asked.

"What about it?"

"It hasn't moved."

"I'll try to find out what's going on."

"Too late," Edith cried out. "It's got to be done now—today!"

"I'm sorry, I'll do everything I can. I promise you that."

After a brief farewell, Victor Monge escorted the Puntarenas visitors to the office front door and out to a busy city street clouded with the sooty, diesel smoke of a passing bus.

Miguel Siboja, Jorge's brother-in-law:
I don't want to make excuses for anyone, but this country doesn't have the money or the means to launch a

big rescue operation. So what happened? Our government, our coast guard, lacked a little logistical sense
here. They should have asked the Americans in Panama
for a little help. They've got the planes and helicopters
and all the equipment you need.

After two or three weeks when the men didn't show up
on the coasts, you could assume they were out on the
high seas. So that's where you look, right? Or at least
try. But that never happened. That was their big error.
They never asked the Americans. That should have been
automatic. If you're not equipped or prepared, you ask
for foreign help. Immediately, especially in an emergency. That's only logical.

But no, they thought they'd rely on local resources.
And what's that? A rickety little plane and maybe one
patrol boat some people say had engine trouble and was
out of order. What kind of an effort is that? That's like
saying, "Go on, boys. You're lost, but who knows, maybe
you'll reach an island or show up on some beach. Go on,
see if you can get out of this by yourselves. You don't
need our help. Be tough, maybe you'll get lucky. Yeah,
that's it. Go to it, boys."

6] LAST CHANCE

After several hours of running for a shore he couldn't see, Gerardo stopped the engine and ordered the sea anchor thrown out. "We're getting nowhere and we're wasting diesel," he told the others in the cabin. "It's no use fighting these waves."

Juan, Pastor, and Jorge, the three who had urged him to spend the last of the fuel heading for the coast, agreed they had no other choice but to stop. For the first time the men spoke openly of salvation and rescue instead of simply help. With only a few gallons of fuel left, they would remain adrift, waiting for a passing ship.

For ten days, until February 11, they drifted in a southwest direction, sighting a number of faraway ships, but none of these responded to the *Cairo*'s signals. Out of flares and not wanting to use any more of their dwindling battery power for the spotlight, they made smoke and fire signals with diesel-soaked rags, towels, shirts, and other clothing. They burned the cloth in a pan and bucket, then climbed on top of the cabin and awning with their flaming beacons. In the daytime they mostly made smoke and steam by slowly burning damp material, but at night they were burning so much material that they switched to pieces of mattress sponge, something they had in greater supply.

Every time a ship was sighted, even if barely visible,

74

they scrambled about doing certain designated duties. Jorge and Juan often took care of preparing the torch, lighting it with sparks made by touching two battery wires together. On the roof the other men waved blankets and pieces of vinyl mattress covering. Once, with the boat rolling and pitching as usual, Pastor sprawled himself on the awning roof, clinging to the edge with one hand and waving a strip of vinyl with the other. "Hey, papa," he shouted to Juan, "watch this!" Pastor rose to his knees, then to his feet, and waved the vinyl with both hands. The wind caught his little banner, pushing him backward and toppling him into the ocean.

Pastor went down with a scream that brought everyone rushing to the stern. He had hit the water about ten feet away and came up floundering.

"Hurry!" Joel yelled, searching the swells for a shark fin.

Pastor started swimming in wild, windmill strokes and quickly reached the boat without the help of a line.

"Hey, clamdigger," Gerardo said as Pastor was helped up, "I thought you were shark food."

Gasping, Pastor lay on the deck, looked up at the amused faces, and smiled. "I was thinking about that too," he said. "And the ship?"

"It's very far," Jorge answered. "They'll never see us."

Pastor raised himself from the deck. "So let's look for another one."

"Just stay dry," Gerardo said flatly, entering the cabin, followed by Joel. "If you die, I've got to answer for a life."

Pastor exchanged glances with Juan and Jorge. "He should have thought of that before the net broke."

"Exactly," Juan said.

"Because of him we're trapped . . . just like shit going down a toilet."

Silent, they gazed at the water until Joel cocked his head toward Pastor, cuffed him gently on the shoulder, and said, "Nice dive."

Joel:
We had decided to leave the boat if we were rescued by a ship. After that one ship left us—the one that came up in the night and put the spotlight on us—well, we cried and kicked ourselves about it. We were so sure they'd pick us up that toward the end, as it got closer, we did nothing. We just stood there like dummies and watched them watching us.

Now, our plan was to put ourselves in the path of some ship, cut in front of it. This time we'd make sure we'd be rescued. We'd make it so they couldn't miss us. The only problem was that our fuel was so low we'd have to wait for a ship to get close enough for us to reach it.

They saw the lights of an airplane only once, in the early evening faraway to the east. It appeared to circle toward them, then it retreated and disappeared. They all saw it, but to Joel it seemed as if the moving lights blended with the reflections on the water. He was squatting by himself on the bow, noticing how the sheen of light under a nearly full moon and clear sky stayed the same despite the sudden, chaotic motions of the water around him. Waves might crash against the boat or a burst of windblown foam might shoot into the air and fall on the surface like sparkling white lace. Yet everything—the sea, the boat, himself—was covered by a soft and steady glow that never changed.

The image of Edith and the girls had that same continual presence in his mind. Whatever was happening at the moment, they were there, watching him, waving hello, offering a kiss, an embrace, always there. He only had to think of living, and Edith and the little ones would crowd around and attach themselves to his neck, arms, and waist. Excited, the girls would shriek in little high voices. Then it would turn quiet and Edith would appear beside him in bed and they would be alone.

On the bow, his back against the cabin just below the windows, Joel shivered from the wind and dampness, looked up at the moon, and began to cry.

During the first two weeks adrift, everyone but Jorge ate some of the dorado strips. "That stuff is putrid," he said. "If I'm going to die, why should I die of indigestion?"

Pastor tried to convince him he wasn't going to die, at least not yet, but the tall, eager kid from the banana coast had become sluggish and indifferent to everything but the possibility of rescue. "You guys can fight the diarrhea, not me."

With the engine stopped, the boat no longer moved faster than the current. Squid and little green fish now gathered alongside and underneath the hull, especially at night, when the cabin lights were on. They dangled a small, plastic cylinder with baitless hooks attached at the end, yanking on the line whenever they felt a tug. For the fish, they used a *chuso*, or spearlike pole that had four, thick, barbed hooks straightened and bound at the end. At first, Joel was the best at using the *chuso*. But once Jorge was roused to eat something other than rotting dorado, he became just as skilled, especially at spearing the smaller fish.

Whatever the amount caught, even a squid the size of a man's hand, Juan tried to cut the pieces in equal sizes, so that later no one would complain of receiving an unfair portion. At first he cooked the pieces by boiling them in saltwater. But since this used up a lot of their cooking gas, he soon shortened the cooking time to a few minutes. "I'll warm up the water," he announced, tossing in a squid, "just enough to knock it out."

By February 11, the current appeared to be carrying them westward, and they were afraid they would be pushed out of the north-south shipping lanes. Their water was also about to run out. For the past week they were each drinking about two cups a day, one in the morning and one at night, and now they were down to their last half-gallon. The men agreed to drink no more than half a cup each, but a few, especially Jorge, felt they were just delaying the inevitable by prolonging their thirst. Why not drink it all now, enjoy every last drop and relieve themselves of this torture? "It's all planned out anyway," Jorge explained. "God has this all figured out. We shouldn't try to change what's happening? If He wants us to die, we die. If we're to be saved, we'll be saved. But let's not fight it."

Juan sided with the young man's fatalism, but Pastor disagreed. "God is making a test for us. Either we pass the test or we don't. What you guys want to do is fail without even trying." They were all slumped around the stern deck, and the rays of a lowering, afternoon sun burned into their unshaded, grizzled faces and grimy bodies.

Gerardo, who usually remained silent during discussions of God and faith, spoke. "The man's right. Every day you stay alive, that's one more day you pass the test."

"All right," Jorge said in a feeble voice. "We drink less. So what?" He got up slowly, grasping an awning post, then moved on wobbly legs toward the cabin, holding on to the rope rail and looking like a baby learning to walk.

"Lazylegs," Joel said, and the others laughed.

Although the swells had decreased in size, allowing the boat to bob with less motion than before, Jorge still couldn't walk without support. For whatever reason—having the longest legs or being a relative novice at sea—Jorge was the most awkward on deck. He boosted himself up onto the cabin roof, caught his breath, then sat to have a look at the horizon. As usual, the wind was starting to pick up. Later in the evening it would blow the hardest, but for now he could sit upright without having to grab the side rails that bordered the rear half of the roof. He scanned the line where sky meets sea, all around, and saw only the immense, white-capped waves beneath a flat, monotonous sky. For a while he listened to Gerardo bail out the engine compartment—lately leaks, not waves, seemed to be causing the flooding. Then he heard Joel tell the others about trying to catch one of the sharks that had come close recently, apparently attracted by the small fish gathered beneath the boat. Finally, about four o'clock, with a dry ache in his throat, Jorge slid his legs over the side of the cabin and was about to let himself down onto the deck when he looked up for one last glance at the horizon. There, toward the south, many miles away, rose two tiny threads of smoke.

"Ships," Jorge cried, pointing. "Two ships!"

The others quickly pulled themselves up for a look. "They're coming this way," Joel said.

"This is it, this is it," Juan shouted. "Thank God, this is it!"

"Wait," Gerardo said, "*three* ships, not two. See the smoke?"

Squinting, they all studied the third smokestack trail.

Juan then climbed down, hurried into the cabin, and started preparing the signal torch.

About fifteen minutes later, as the ships drew within a mile to two miles of the *Cairo*, Jorge stood on the bow and began waving a blanket. "How can we miss?" he said. "One of them has to stop."

After a few more minutes it was apparent that the first two ships, which were freighters, would pass by about a half-mile west of them. But the third ship, which had a black hull and looked like an oil tanker, would come within a hundred yards east of their boat.

"What'll we do?" Joel asked Gerardo.

"We wait."

Juan asked about moving closer to the black ship, but the others agreed it wouldn't be necessary. The giant tanker would come so close that they wouldn't have to start the engine. Meanwhile, they all turned their attention to the first two ships. Joel stood on top of the cabin, holding the smoking bits of cloth and mattress sponge, moving the whole mess from side to side. The others hung on at the bow or stern yelling and waving shirts, blankets, and sheets of vinyl or canvas. And above, at the rear of the awning, a Costa Rican flag the size of a dish towel fluttered from a long, nailed-on stick.

The first two freighters passed, but not before the men had a chance to shout the usual obscenities to the unknown, unaware persons inside. However, they weren't too frustrated, since they knew the third ship was about to pass right next to them.

"Get ready, boys," Pastor announced gleefully. "Here she comes."

Wide, long, and riding low in the water, the massive black shape was mostly flat on top, except for the superstructure at the stern. The men of the *Cairo* shouted and signaled, their screams ever more desperate. The tanker

was about eighty yards away, and it was as if no one were
on watch in the bridge, or everyone asleep; the ship
might as well be steering itself, indifferent to the frantic
human forms below and off the port side.

Just then a door opened and a man appeared outside
on the bridge wing. At first he didn't see the five, but he
must have heard their shouts because he turned his head
sharply in their direction, peered at them, then rushed
back into the bridge. Seconds later, he reappeared, this
time with another man, who focused on them with binoculars. Soon other crewmen were on the bridge and below
on the main deck, some looking perplexed, others waving a greeting.

The *Cairo* crew kept up their commotion, screaming to
be heard above the wind and the deep drone of the
tanker's engines. For several minutes, the tanker crew,
who appeared to be Asian, were intently watchful. But
the ship never slowed, leaving behind the five frenzied
figures shrieking and begging for help. They cried and
cursed, fell to their knees, and pleaded with open arms.
But the giant vessel kept moving. Joel cleared his eyes
and made out the words *Clipper Nissau* on the stern.

"Wait," Jorge said, "I think it's turning."

"It is," Pastor whispered. "Yes, it's turning. They're
coming back!"

Another twenty minutes passed by the time the tanker
doubled back, making another giant U-turn to come up
and stop within forty yards of the *Cairo*. Before the boat
could drift away, a crewman aboard the *Clipper* threw
out a line with a small weight attached at the end. It
landed about twenty-five feet from the bow of the *Cairo*,
bobbing on the surface in fifteen-foot swells. While the
tanker crewman retrieved the line, Pastor hurried up from
the stern and tied a bow-line around his waist. "Look,"
he told Gerardo, "next time when they throw out the

line, I'll jump in and swim for it. Watch out for the sharks. After I get it, pull me in—hard!"

Gerardo, who was climbing down from the cabin roof, was about to answer Pastor when Joel and Juan started shouting for him to move the boat closer. "Start the engine! Now's our chance! Hurry! Start it, start it! We've got one gallon left—use it!"

Hearing their pleas, Pastor rushed back to the stern and entered the cabin where the other four had gathered around the engine, which could be started with a crank handle if the battery-powered starter failed to work. "Are you guys crazy or what?" Pastor screamed. "Don't turn it on. They think our engine's dead. So leave it like that."

"Turn it on!"

"No! They've started their maneuver, they want to rescue us."

"Start it! We're wasting time."

"Start it and they'll think we're not in trouble."

"Gerardo," Juan cried hysterically, "do something! Get this piece of junk moving."

For a moment Gerardo appeared confused by the babble of voices and suggestions. "Hell, let's just get the line," he muttered.

"Yes, yes, start the engine," Juan insisted, his hands on the crank handle.

"I'm telling you, don't start it," Pastor said.

"He's right," Jorge added. "We agreed not to start it."

Gerardo looked at Pastor with a disgusted expression. The smaller man then threw up a hand. "Hell, do what you want," he said, and left to return to the bow. He hoped the engine would not start, but once he was outside, he heard it start with a pop on the first crank. The boat lurched forward, and with Gerardo spinning the wheel, they turned and moved toward the tanker.

When they were within twenty yards of the black hull, Gerardo cut the engine, and this time they easily caught the line thrown out to them. Pastor and Juan quickly tied it to one of the awning posts, and Joel climbed up on the cabin roof. The only Asians the *Cairo* crew had known in Costa Rica were Chinese, and they believed the tanker crewmen were Chinese.

"Joel, you talk to the Chinese," Gerardo shouted from below.

Joel became the designated spokesman and translator, since he once said he knew a little English. Gerardo figured if the Chinese didn't speak Spanish, maybe they knew English.

Alongside the giant tanker near the stern, the *Cairo* looked like a rowboat, rising and falling on the swells that hardly moved the ship up or down. On the tanker, one of the dozen or so men standing at the rail on the main deck cupped his hands to his mouth and shouted in Spanish, "What's wrong?"

Joel explained they were in trouble. A storm had blown them away from the coast, they were out of fuel, and they desperately needed help. For emphasis, he even said they had been adrift one month, although it had only been seventeen days since the net broke. Sobbing, he pleaded with the crew to rescue them.

But the crewman who had called out to them did not understand what Joel was saying. Over and over, Joel tried to make himself clear until finally he blurted the word "water" in English.

"Water?" the crewman repeated, then gave an order to the others and soon a hose was thrown across. Pastor caught it and Gerardo told Juan to start filling the forty-five-gallon water barrel on board.

"Mexico? Mexico?" the same crewman called.

"No," Joel answered, "Costa Rica."

"Ah, Costa Rica," the man said, and pointed west. "Twenty miles," he added in English, "twenty miles!"

Joel translated this, then Gerardo said to ask for diesel. Holding up an empty fuel can, Joel repeated the word "diesel" until the crewman motioned for him to toss the can across to them. Timing his throw so that the cabin roof would be raised even with the deck on the next swell, Joel heaved it across with a line attached to the handle. The crewmen caught it, untied the line, and carried it away.

Suddenly a uniformed man on the bridge wing began shouting orders. He appeared to be the captain, since the crew responded immediately, motioning for the *Cairo* crew to release the line, again calling out unintelligible words. Above, the captain shook his head and made angry gestures toward both crews. By now Joel realized the captain had decided not to rescue them.

Hoping to stall the other crew until the *Cairo*'s water tank was filled, Pastor offered them dorado strips, which they refused.

After the fuel can was returned, the two crews began a brief tug-of-war with the tanker line that was attached to the awning post. Finally, the water hose was yanked back. Then, afraid the post would break from the strain on the line, Jorge and Pastor started to untie it. That's when Joel, again timing the rise and fall of the boat so that he would be level with the ship's deck, readied himself to jump across. Just as he was about to leap, the tanker crewmen—encouraged by their captain's shouts—raised their arms to push him back. In vain Joel begged them to let him jump aboard. But with the line and hose pulled back, the tanker's engines started up and the ship slowly began to pull away. Several of the tanker crew were crying and gesturing to the bridge, as if to say they were sorry but they were only following orders.

The screams from the *Cairo* continued until the tanker was far beyond hearing range. Finally the men slumped to the deck, spent and stunned.

"So stupid," Juan sputtered in disgust. "We're idiots."

"Be quiet," Pastor said.

Joel lifted his head from his chest. "How was it possible? We had life so close and it slipped through our hands."

For a long while they were silent. Then Pastor slapped the cabin side, gestured with his head toward Gerardo, and announced, "It's his fault. I told the son of a bitch not to start the engine. I told him, I told him, I told him."

Gerardo picked up a knife that was stuck in the deck between his legs, stabbed a nearby piece of dorado, and with a steady hand placed the putrid meat on his tongue. No one spoke as they watched him slowly chew and then swallow. For a long time he stared at the retreating speck on the darkening horizon.

Gerardo:

I don't know, we had no reason to do it, to start the engine. But everyone was shouting to do it, to do it . . . That was our last good chance, and we failed. From then on, all that was left was to keep on fighting. All I could think of was the diesel. The *Clipper* gave us kerosene, not diesel. What good was that? And there was no coast twenty miles away. We might as well have been a thousand miles away. That night there were no lights or anything in the west, so how did they come up with twenty miles? But Joel spoke to the Chinese, and that's what he said they said.

After the *Clipper* left us, that's when our situation got ugly. We didn't expect to see any more ships. We were on our own. It was up to God now . . . and wherever the wind wanted to take us.

7] SEPARATE QUARTERS

Joel's dream took him back to Costa Rica, to the main shipping port, Puerto Caldera. The *Cairo III* had finished its fishing trip and was finally returning. As the boat moved through the calm water toward the wharf, Joel noticed they were suddenly in the shadow of the *Clipper* oil tanker. A voice called from above and Joel saw a lone figure leaning over the deck rail.

It was the Chinese crewman who hadn't understood him. He was now speaking in smooth Spanish. Joel listened to him apologize for not rescuing them, but orders were orders. He said he felt bad about the whole thing because he could see Joel and the others with him were in some kind of trouble. But it was never clear.

In the dream, Joel explained about the mistake they had made in starting the engine. The crewman then said that his captain didn't like being fooled, and that it looked like the Costa Ricans were only pretending to be in trouble. Or they might even be pirates or thieves. The captain had to be careful.

But Joel said they were just fishermen, and they were hungry and thirsty, and they were almost out of fuel. Couldn't his captain see that they were desperate men begging for help?

The Chinese crewman again said he was sorry, then added, "I just want you to know one thing: we would have saved you, but you started the engine. That was your mistake. You shouldn't have started the engine."

February 16:
   After their near-rescue by the oil tanker, the men of the *Cairo III* saw one more vessel. In the morning light, they could clearly discern the giant letters H-Y-U-N-D-A-I emblazoned across the side of the long hull. They made the usual fire and smoke signals, even trying to attract attention with the reflection from a small mirror. But the container ship continued north, giving no sign of having seen the hapless fishermen.
   After the ship passed and they were in the cabin, Joel sourly concluded, "This is hopeless. What good is all our screaming and everything if nobody sees us?"
   "Maybe they'll radio somebody to help us," Jorge said.
   "You're dreaming. Don't you think the *Clipper* would have done that for us?"
   "He's right, Lazylegs," Pastor said. "Forget ships. We had our big chance and we lost it—no, *he* lost it."
   Gerardo, who was on his knees checking the water level rising around the engine, appeared not to have heard the remark. He rose and wiped his dripping hands on his chest and thighs. "We're going to sink," he began, "unless we bail. And I mean all the time. The leaks are getting worse, and if the borers break through, we're finished."
   They decided to bail in two-man teams every two hours. Three men would rest while two bailed, one to scoop water and lift the pail from below the deck, and the other to dump it overboard or through the stern-deck scuppers. They would rotate the duty day and night. All five agreed to the arrangement, and though Gerardo gave the order, his approval no longer seemed to matter.

Among themselves, the crewmen began to mutter sneering insults about the captain, wishing they had fought him on his early decisions.

Of their two tanks of cooking gas, one was empty and the other nearly empty. The batteries were useless, and they had no more electricity or diesel fuel—so the bilge pump wouldn't work. The only positive note was their continuing skill in snagging squid and a little green and red newcomer they called a rainbow fish.

In the afternoon Juan dropped the chopped and washed pieces in a pot of seawater, warmed the mixture, and called it a Sea Stew Deluxe. It wasn't much more than a few mouthfuls, but as their single daily meal, it was at least palatable. Even Jorge, who refused the dorado, wanted more.

In the afternoon, while three men rested under the awning and the other two bailed, a plump, big-billed booby swooped down over the boat, then plopped down to ride the swells about thirty yards away. Later the nonbailers watched the black long-necked shapes of a few cormorants diving for prey. Occasionally they glimpsed a black-tipped shark fin or saw a blunt-headed dorado flash out of the water behind a flying fish, its tiny form flitting and banking just out of reach.

After it grew dark, long after sunset, everyone stayed in the bunks except the two dumping the water off the deck. The bailing duo worked by touch, since, except for a luminescent watch dial, the cabin was completely black to the eye. With a slice of moon visible in the cloudless sky, the only brightness came from the stars and sometimes a phosphorescent streak in the breaking waves.

"Hyundai, huh?" someone said.

"Like the car."

"What is that, Japanese?"

"Chinese, Japanese, what difference does it make?"

"Calm down."

"You calm down."

"Go to sleep."

"I can't."

"I can't either."

"Well, just shut up."

"Whenever I'm hungry, I can't sleep."

"Juan, you think you're alone?"

"I'm hungry."

"Ohhh, and what would Your Ancientness like to eat?"

"Go to hell."

"Pudding? How about chocolate pudding? Rich and sweet, with a little swirl on top?"

"Shut up!"

"How about some cookies and some cake?"

"Stop it!"

"Hey, leave the old man alone."

"Why should I? Is he the only one who's hungry?"

"Well, lay off, so maybe we can sleep."

"All right, all right . . . let the old goat sleep."

That night no one slept well or for very long. When they weren't bailing, they lay in their bunks listening to the clanking sound of the bailing pail, waiting for the slap of each successive wave against the hull, hearing and feeling the boat shudder, its every timber, plank, and joint chafing, twisting, creaking, again and again.

Gerardo:

You don't think I worried? All I thought about was them and the boat and how long we could stay alive out here if we had to. What if we started sinking? What would we do? I started thinking of how long it would take to sink. I could see the leaks in the seams and the water pouring in. It was like a nightmare, except it was real. Everyday I just had to look and I could see it was filling up faster. Without the pump, we had to bail. All of us, that was the rule. We argued about a lot of things, but there was never a question about bailing. We just did it. It was either bail the water or sink and die.

February 19:

Now located about nine degrees latitude north of the equator, the men found relief from the suffocating midday heat by pouring seawater over their heads. The cool dousings were the only breaks they took from the continuous bailing and lookout duty for fish. Three days had passed without sighting a ship, so they no longer scanned the horizon regularly, believing they had drifted out of the coastal lanes days ago. They didn't bother to throw out the old tire as a sea anchor.

The situation looked grim but there were a few positives. The swells had dropped in height, the gusts had changed to a steady breeze, and they calculated they had about two weeks' drinking water left. With the flooding more or less controlled by bailing, their remaining big problem was a lack of food. For three days they hadn't eaten anything more than teasing bits of squid, and they were achingly hungry. Drooped over the sides, listless, they spent most of the day watching the rise and fall of the water's blue-green surface, hoping to spot something to spear or snag.

Then the little shape appeared. It was about the size of a small duck, but to the five underfed men the grayish-green turtle paddling some ten yards away looked like a floating banquet.

"How do we catch it?" Joel asked, setting down the spearlike *chuso* tipped with the barbed, straightened hooks.

Pastor reached for a coil of nylon fishing line. "We'll hook him," he said, and while the others watched, he attached a few lead weights on the line inches above a

hook the size of an average safety pin. Then he tossed
the weighted line toward his target. On the second throw,
the hook snagged a fold of the loose, leathery skin of the
turtle's neck.

"That's it, little turtle," Pastor coaxed, "come to papa,
come to papa." Gently he tugged the line, then played it
out and in as the animal wriggled and dipped its head,
trying to free itself of the hook. When the turtle came
alongside the boat, Gerardo took over, grabbing one of
the claw-tipped flippers. The captain caught the nearest
front flipper with one hand and lifted the turtle out of the
water, over the side, and onto the deck.

While the crew watched, he unsnagged the hook and
asked for a knife. Then with the turtle sighing loudly on
its back, Gerardo thrust the six-inch blade under the
hard bottom near the neck. In one deft, seesaw motion,
he punctured the heart. Next, he severed the thick skin
around the edge where the shell meets the flat yellow
bottom and removed it, exposing the bowl-shaped cavity
filled with dark entrails, purplish organs, and puddles of
blood. Gerardo tilted the shell and spilled the blood onto
the deck. Then he cut away the heart, lungs, kidneys,
and liver, handing them one by one to the four spectators
to be thrown away. Finally, he sliced off the nubby tail
and the glistening pink meat at the shoulders and pelvic
area, dropping everything else—head, shell, entrails, and
flippers—over the side.

For the moment, Gerardo was a hero, an expert wres-
tler of turtles, a master with the knife.

"Let's celebrate," Joel suggested.

"Let's just eat," said Juan, entering the cabin.

"This is our first birthday. We've been gone one month."

"Fine," came Juan's voice from inside, "let's celebrate."

About an hour later, the bandy-legged cook emerged
with a covered pot. "I made a surprise," he said with a

grin. Then he removed the top and watched the other four lean forward to inspect the steamy contents. "I saved a little of the rice—you know, for something special."

"You're a gentleman," Gerardo said, and they all retrieved their spoons and cups or bowls from the cabin.

Juan served out the portions, and they sat on the deck and began to eat. Only Jorge balked at eating turtle, saying it would make him sick.

Although they finished the watery mixture in ten or fifteen minutes, the spirit of the feast lasted the entire afternoon. They stopped bailing and for a while seemed to forget their misery, savoring the taste of the rice, which reminded them of their families and friends. Eastward, toward their home in Costa Rica, the sky was gray and becoming dark, but toward the west, where they preferred to look, the sky was lit in a brilliant blend of orange and red spreading itself out from the descending sun, huge and shimmering.

Gerardo:

I forgot my picky tastes. The secret to eating anything, even rotten, stinking food, is hunger. If you've never felt that kind of hunger, you won't understand. Not really. I used to be so delicate about what I would and would not eat. Poor Lidia, she'd have to make everything special for me. Well, all that changed once I decided I wasn't going to die from hunger. Not when there was something to eat. I became like a dog. I'd eat anything. I wouldn't even smell it. Whatever it was, I'd get it down. I just wouldn't think about it. If it's really bad, like those putrid pieces of dorado, you stop smelling and tasting because all you want to do is fill your belly.

That turtle and rice was really special. We made it a party. We just sat back and enjoyed the moment. I couldn't have been happier. Nobody was angry, nobody argued, nobody was blaming me for this thing or that thing. We were just relaxing and hanging on to the taste of rice, knowing it was our last.

Then, as the sun went down, we started talking about home. The guys were going on about their wives and kids and sisters and brothers, on and on about how their families must be suffering. "No," I said. "We're the ones suffering the most. They're walking around on land, they're safe. We're the ones who are screwed. You guys shouldn't be thinking about them. Just worry about yourselves."

Then I told them I had a dream that all five of us would get out of this mess together, alive, and that nobody was going to die.

"Yeah," Pastor said, "let's set a record for being lost out here."

"Dead or alive?" somebody asked.

It was a joke, that's all, and everybody laughed.

Gerardo noted the day, Friday, on the face of his watch. "Not a very productive week," he said.

"What are you proposing?" Joel asked.

"Nothing. Only an observation."

"Then why don't we do something, like put up a real sail?" Pastor said. "You know, with a mast and all."

Since the rain usually came up from the south, maybe they should put up a sail and head in that direction. With the north wind pushing them from behind, they could easily head south.

No one knew for sure what lay south—islands here and there, South America vaguely off to the west, remembered images of an immense blue space on the maps and globes they could recall. But they were all certain the rainy season would begin soon and that the showers usually came from the south.

Gerardo asked Juan if a good sail could be put up with what they had on the boat.

"I'll think about it," the former sailor answered. "No, wait, I'll draw it." Using a pencil and piece of paper, he sketched a crude outline of a mast, sail, and boom rising above a boxy outline of the *Cairo III*. Juan lifted his head, smiling, and said, "Yes, we can do it."

February 20:

Not long after sunrise, someone calmly said, "Let's do it, let's tear down the cabin." The decision was spontaneous. As usual, Jorge at first refused to participate. The most cautious and timid of the five, he argued they would lose their protection. What would happen to them in another storm? What about the cold at night?

The idea was to dismantle the main part of the cabin to clear a space for a mast and boom, made with the roof cross beams. For a sail, they would stitch together blankets and pieces of the vinyl with wire and fishing line. Then they would make a tiller and rudder with plywood and planks. Only the front section of the cabin would remain to serve as a base support for the twelve-foot-high mast, made with three overlapping beams. The rest of the salvaged wood would be used for cooking, since their butane gas was low.

Gerardo led the assault with the boat's only hammer, the others with pipes and heavy wrenches. They tore away the bunks, smashed the galley counter, and knocked out the side windows and walls. Like ants destroying their nest, they attacked every support, beam, and plank with a zeal they hadn't felt for weeks. At last they were active, focused, swinging their weapons like men breaking out of prison. After a while, even a grumbling Jorge joined the fray.

Only the thick heavy roof stymied them; too many

nails and screws held it together. They were lodged everywhere, and the men repeatedly cursed the builder for his thoroughness.

At one point Gerardo whacked his finger and had to give up the hammer to Pastor, who immediately delivered a roundhouse bash to a stubborn corner of the roof. Gerardo was about to tell him to tie the handle to his hand when Pastor lost his grip on the handle and the hammer flew out over the water. No one reproached him at the time, but from their glances he knew they were angry at his carelessness.

Later, as they removed the unusable roof to toss it overboard, Pastor spotted a skinny rat hiding in a hollow space under the roof. It jumped into the water, but Pastor grabbed a makeshift gaff and hooked the animal before it had gone too far from the boat. Gripping the rat with both hands, he struck it against the deck, cracking its neck. Then he stripped away the hairy skin with a knife and ate the exposed, scrawny flesh.

The other men hardly noticed Pastor's ravenous attack on the rat. They continued enthusiastically prying away boards and planks, expecting, perhaps hoping, another rat would burst from its hiding spot. But none did, and the five completed the dismantling by midmorning. With the wood neatly stacked up on each side of the engine, the boat's profile now resembled a fat gondola with a four-poster awning at the stern and a boothlike piece of the cabin at the bow.

Joel:

The boat was a floating hardware store. Nails and screws everywhere. But as soon as we finished ripping apart the cabin, Juan was up making the mast. I guess the old man was good for something, after all. He designed the whole thing, but we helped him nail and tie things together. At first the rudder didn't work so well because it was too short. So Gerardo made one that went deeper, and that seemed to do it. The next day, when we finally put up the little sail and actually started moving, I think we were all amazed. The whole thing worked, we were going south. The wind wasn't as strong anymore, but at least it hit us from behind, and off we went, looking for rain.

About that time, things had started to change. I mean among the five of us. Ever since the *Clipper* episode, there had been no leadership. We swore that if we got another chance at being rescued, this time we'd do the right thing. But we'd actually given up on seeing another ship. So, naturally, we blamed Gerardo. He was the captain, he was the responsible one. It didn't matter that we might have influenced him to do something. The fact is he made the decisions.

We were angry and we showed it. From now on, all of us would make decisions as a group. If we failed, we would all fail, all of us would share the blame.

Gerardo became just another one of the crew. Some of us said he was even less than that. No, we weren't going to trust him with our lives anymore.

At first I didn't think it affected him. He probably thought it was a necessary arrangement. Besides, what could he do about it? It was four against one. Then one night, right after we put up the sail, he tried to sleep in the icebox with us. There wasn't much room left, so he went off to sleep in the bow.

Maybe he felt guilty or upset with himself about what had happened so far. Among the four of us we talked about it a lot, and some of us would throw it in his face. But whatever he felt, he never let on, never answered us. Just kept quiet. From then on, he stayed at his end of the boat. Most of the time, that's where he was. He slept in the bow, and we slept in the icebox.

He made a little space for himself in the bow, and you could see it wasn't very protected. I'm sure he was colder and wetter than where we were. At least we could cover the icebox. But Gerardo couldn't do anything except wait till the sun came up. But that's what he chose. He wanted to be alone. It was almost like he was punishing himself.

February 23:

They caught three small sharks with a hook attached to a short length of wire, tied to several nylon fishing lines. Before using the wire, the sharks had taken most of their hooks. Now they only had two hooks left, and the men carefully handled and stored them on the deck.

Pastor became the cook because he was the most adept at using the Bic lighter and not wasting the fluid. With no matches and the batteries dropped overboard, the Bic was the only way to start a cooking fire. And though the meat was often only warmed, the men insisted on having cooked meals. They cooked on a hibachilike stove they had made by cutting away the top of the empty butane tank, punching holes near the bottom, and putting a metal grill on top. Pastor used the gas in the other tank to light the kindling, and as long as the wood and Bic fluid lasted, the men expected a fire.

The nonstop bailing continued, but without the cabin in the way, one man was enough for the task, now done in four-hour rotating shifts. However, with a sail came the added duty of keeping the boat on course. So they agreed there should also be a four-hour shift at the tiller. All told, they were on duty eight of every twenty-four hours.

Gerardo had his say on matters, like throwing over the

heavy diesel fuel tank to lighten the boat. But mostly he kept his silence, remaining separate as much as possible.

As they sailed south, there was still no sign of rain or clouds. Even with severe rationing, Joel calculated they only had about two weeks' worth of drinking water. In the afternoon, figuring they might run out of water before finding rain, he decided to drop an unused metal container overboard. Maybe it would drift ashore somewhere, maybe a ship would see it. If they were lucky, someone might find it, and there, scratched on the side, would be Joel's message: "*Cairo III,* Puntarenas, Costa Rica. If this is found, please inform officials that a buoy was found. We have fifteen days of water left. February 23, 1988."

8] PANDORA

"Is it true Papi's dead?" Sharon asked, pulling on her mother's sleeve.

Edith was kneeling in prayer in the washing room at the rear of the house. Dozens of slender little candles, some of them lit, were stuck on the cement floor next to a roller-top washer.

"Is it true?"

"Sharon, not now."

Edith's eldest child watched the tiny flames, waiting while the Our Fathers continued. Her mother's eyes were closed, hands clasped under her chin. Somewhere a radio announced a pill to relieve headaches, next door a woman's voice was calling a goat, and at the front of the house, Lila barked at somebody through the fence.

Sharon stepped closer, eye level with her mother. "They said he drowned."

Edith opened her eyes. "Who said?"

"The kids at school."

Edith embraced her daughter. "Don't believe them. They don't know what they're saying."

"They said he's not coming back."

Edith wiped away Sharon's tears. "He'll be back, don't you worry. He hasn't drowned, and he's alive. Now, go play with your sisters. I'm almost done."

After Sharon left, Edith felt an even greater urgency in

praying for Joel's return. Her own mother told her not to expect the government to save the men. Only prayers could help bring them home, especially prayers to the Holy Child of Prague, savior of lost souls. Joel and the others were alive—struggling but alive—and Edith must not lose hope.

Edith's mother, Alicia, had herself been told by a spiritist that the men were alive. Sitting at a table with a glass of water between them, Alicia joined hands with the old man, who recited prayers and invoked Joel's name. Alicia was instructed to look closely at the water's surface; then, with the spiritist coaxing her, she saw Joel in miniature, clinging to a floating piece of wood near the bow of the boat. Then he let go of the wood and appeared to be swimming.

"I would have asked you along," she later told Edith, "but I didn't want to alarm you. What if we saw him dead or something? Now we know he's alive."

Besides her mother's vision, there were also the dreams that Joel was alive. Her second-youngest daughter, Tracy, for example, once came to her crying in the middle of the night. She had dreamed of her father. He entered her room, sat beside her on the bed, and gave her lots of candies. Then he picked her up and gave her two small fish. That's when Tracy woke up crying because just the sight and touch of cold, scaly fish always made her sick.

Edith explained to her pixie-faced daughter that her father only wanted to give her a present and that he must have forgotten how she felt about fish. "At least he's thinking of you," Edith said. "He's trying to be nice."

It was now nearing the end of February and no major effort had been made to search for the men. Edith and Lidia had gone to San José several times to visit Victor Monge, their sympathetic contact in the Foreign Relations Ministry. His telegrams to authorities in other countries produced only polite but negative responses—there were no signs of the *Cairo III* and its crew. On the slight chance that the boat was drifting thousands of miles west, Monge even asked the Costa Rican consul in Hawaii to inform the U.S. Coast Guard of the *Cairo*'s disappearance.

The two wives thanked Monge for his help, then launched an information campaign of their own. They made their plea to the newspapers and radio stations; stories appeared and interviews with them were broadcast. Why were their men being abandoned by the government? Why wasn't a proper search-and-rescue effort carried out? Every day the coast guard waited was another day lost, another day in which the men could be found. The longer the government waited, the slimmer the chances were they'd be found at all.

Buoyed by the publicity, Edith and Lidia thought they should climb another rung in the bureaucratic ladder. They would meet with the vice-minister in charge of the coast guard. And this time they would bolster their case by convincing the *Cairo*'s owner, Carlos Rohmán, to accompany them. So far, he had begged off the San José visits, complaining he was sick.

In Puntarenas again, they were now entering Rohmán's house. As usual he sat in his living-room rocking chair smoking a cigarette. A large black-and-white picture of the *Cairo III*—named with his Egyptian, immigrant forebears in mind—lay in view on a nearby cabinet.

"You watch, he'll have an excuse," Lidia whispered.

After they were seated, Edith said they had an appointment to meet the vice-minister in a few days. "We want you to go with us."

The boat owner looked annoyed but saw that they

looked determined. "Who's going to speak for the group?" he asked.

"You are."

"What?"

"You can also arrange the trip."

"Oh, no, that's not my respon—"

"Just a minute," Edith interrupted, eyes ablaze. "This *is* your responsibility. It's your boat and your crew. We're just the wives and we'll go with you. But please, Don Carlos, you must do the talking."

"Ladies, this has been very hard on me."

Edith shook her head. "And us? You think you're the only one sick?"

"I didn't say that."

"We're all sick! Please don't start with that I'm-not-feeling-well stuff. All of us are suffering—mothers, wives, sisters, children."

"Gerardo and Joel are like sons to me."

"It's not the same!"

"Lower your voice."

"My voice is fine."

"Maybe we should talk some other time."

"No!"

"You're hysterical."

"No, sir," Edith snapped, glaring at the man's florid face through the layers of smoke. "No, *I'm* not hysterical—*you're* the one who's hysterical."

Lidia spoke. "Don Carlos, we'll be here at eight o'clock on the day of the appointment."

"That's too early. I sleep late."

"Well," Edith said, "you'll just have to get up early for a change."

Rohmán lit another cigarette, inhaled, and blew a little gray cloud above their heads. "Look," he said, "I can give you both some money to help at home."

Edith made a futile wave at the smoke. "We didn't come here for money. Let's not talk about money. You think money will solve our problems?"

"We just want our men back," Lidia added. "We want our husbands."

Edith stood and abruptly extended a hand through the

"Of course, of course," he said, frowning in thought.

Vice-minister Rogelio Castro, a large, gray-haired man, met the Puntarenas visitors in an elegant third-floor office in downtown San José. As the group's reluctant spokesman, Carlos Rohmán quickly explained the reason for their visit.

Castro then spoke, sympathizing with their situation and apologizing that some of the coast-guard boats were in bad condition and had not been able to do a thorough search. "For now, we've done all we can. You see, we just don't have the money to be out looking for a boat we don't know will ever appear."

Until now, Edith had kept silent out of respect for the vice-minister's position. But she could no longer contain herself, finally interrupting. "How can you say that? How do you know they won't appear unless you try to find them?"

Rohmán and a few relatives of the lost men gestured for Edith to quiet down, but she continued, growing angrier. "The government spends thousands on fuel to go out cruising to different islands. So why can't they spend that money looking for our men? Why isn't the government doing something?"

The vice-minister nodded, trying to control his irritation at the young woman's onslaught. "You're right," he said. "We could have done more. All I can say is that we'll keep trying with the means we have."

Edith was silent during the rest of the twenty-minute meeting, afraid that she would be rude if she spoke.

On the drive home in Rohmán's car, she sat in the rear with Lidia. Their faces were smeared with tears. "What good was all that?" Edith said. "He doesn't care."

"Well," Lidia said, blowing her nose, "he said he'd send some planes out."

"Yeah, like last time. No, he won't do anything. Why should he? We're nothing to him."

Later, before they arrived in Puntarenas, Lidia asked, "What, now?"

Without hesitating, Edith replied, "Enough vice-minister—let's go see the minister!"

Many years ago, a psychologist and clairvoyant named Moreno Caña lived in Costa Rica. Revered as a wise man, he especially helped the poor with physical and spiritual problems. After he died, his presence continued in the guise of others who claimed Moreno Caña spoke to them telepathically. One such person, a man in his forties, was in Puntarenas in February and March to help people consult with the renowned seer. Edith's mother requested a telepathic session.

Speaking in a strange, deep voice that didn't sound like his own, the man said, "Tell your daughter not to worry. The men are alive."

As Alicia later explained to her daughter, the voice of Moreno Caña said he had trouble locating the five survivors because telepathic contact over water is difficult. But despite the vagueness of the vision, he could see they were approaching a small, uninhabited island covered with jagged peaks of rock. He believed the name of this islet was Pandora. He wasn't sure but he thought Pandora was located off the coast of Panama.

"Don't lose hope," the voice said. "But don't get too

excited. They aren't safe yet. It looks as if the boat is still holding up. But if a big storm hits them, they won't last."

Edith and Lidia asked everyone who would listen if they had heard of Pandora. They informed Don Carlos and the coast-guard station, and they searched maps, globes, and charts. No one knew of the island, no atlas listed the name. The only reference they could find was to the Greek myth about Pandora, the first-created woman and the one who released from a small box all of mankind's evils. In some versions, the box contained blessings, all of which escaped except hope. The two wives ignored any bleak significance of the name, insisting only on finding the mysterious island.

In early March, Edith began making calls to San José for an audience with the minister. Getting an appointment would take time, she was told. Meanwhile, she and Lidia began to wander the streets like sleepwalkers, leaving their children with relatives and friends, continually asking fishermen and anyone connected with the sea if they had word about the *Cairo* and its crew. A fishing cooperative and several neighbors, though poor themselves, donated small amounts of food and money to both women and to Pastor's wife, Rita. The contributions helped, but as the days passed, more people started treating them as widows, suggesting the men's survival was now impossible.

Only briefly did their sense of helplessness fade. This occurred after another local fishing boat, the *Dragón 2,* was reported lost just north of the *Cairo III*'s last fishing site. The owners of the *Dragón 2* were a relatively wealthy, local Chinese family, and they chartered a plane that searched the area for many hours. The women of the *Cairo* crew hoped the plane would spot their own men, but after repeated flights neither boat was sighted.

Other than this, the only activity that might lead to a rescue were the frequent radio broadcasts by the coast guard and one commercial station. Destined for passing ships and aircraft, the message now concerned two missing boats.

About a month and a half after the *Cairo* was reported missing, Joel's normally frisky Doberman, not much more than a pup, stopped barking. One afternoon Lila became listless and silent. Then she wouldn't eat. She lay around whimpering and crying. Edith's father, who was home between cruise-ship tours, first tried feeding the dog bread soaked in milk, then a milk-and-lemon-juice mixture. He rubbed her legs, massaged her stomach, held her in his arms, and spoke to her. Nothing worked. Lila remained quiet throughout the night.

The next morning, Edith discovered the dog's motionless body in the backyard next to the canal. Lila was facing the water, head between her paws, dried blood on one side of her mouth.

"She was waiting for Papi," Edith told the girls after they buried Lila in a corner of the yard. "She always waited for him by the water, looking at the boats."

"Somebody poisoned her," Edith's father said.

Edith looked surprised. "How do you know?"

"She scared people."

"So?"

"People get mad, think the dog's evil or something."

"Lila never hurt the girls. Why would someone poison her?"

"Maybe she bit someone."

Edith told her daughters Lila died from sadness because Joel hadn't come home. He'd been gone too long and the dog missed her best friend.

"But he is coming home, isn't he?" Tracy asked.

"Of course," Edith said.

"He's alive?"

"Yes. You see him in your dreams, remember?"

"It's not the same."

"Well, almost."

Tracy was adamant, shaking her head. "He wouldn't give me those stinking fish."

"You're right, my love."

"Papi wouldn't give me fish."

"Never."

"Not the same."

Edith smiled. "No, a dream is not the same."

9] THE ISLAND

Gerardo:

I was a nothing. Whatever the others said, fine, fine—I'd go along with it. I didn't want problems, didn't want to start arguments. What for? That got us nowhere. It was better to keep quiet, stay away from them as much as I could, mind my own business.

If they were talking about something, I wouldn't say a word. I'd just stay in my place in the bow and listen to them at their end, going on and on, arguing and cussing about this and that. If they asked me something, I'd say, "Whatever you guys decide, fine." I'd listen to their opinions and that's all. They didn't want my opinion anyway.

But whatever they decided, I'd join in and help. That's the way I am. I want to do something and I do it—boom, right away. If things don't turn out right, well, too bad. I keep going, I don't give up. Like the sail. Someone said, "Let's do it," and we did it. If you feel something's right, why go on thinking about it? So we tore down the cabin and made the sail. It took us two or three days, and then, bam, we were off sailing south—finally doing something, running somewhere. We didn't know where, but at least we were running.

The trouble was, they changed their minds. I went along, but I thought it was strange. We'd only been sailing a few days and they wanted to change direction. They wanted to make another run for the coast. So fine, we changed our direction. But I told them, "You thought of this, not me. You came up with the idea of going south. Now you want to go east. All right, whatever you want."

I didn't say much, but I knew something very different was happening because after we got started, one by one, they came up with the idea of not working.

The leak around the screw in the forward part of the keel made a constant gurgling, whooshing sound. It was the worst of all the leaks, and since it was located beneath Gerardo's sleeping spot in the bow, he heard it the most. Whenever he lay down, it was there, in his thoughts, sometimes in his dreams. There, near the upturned part of the keel, with every wave that hit the boat, he heard the corroded piece of metal twisting and wrenching itself loose in the rotting wood. In the dark, he had memorized its feel, the bolt at the top, the mushy, ragged wood around the head. He knew its sounds, knew just by listening if the water was spurting or gushing, running or seeping. So he squirmed himself in between the deck and the hull and repeatedly plugged the leak with bits of sponge, rope, and cloth. But the wood was so soft that Gerardo could plug only gently, afraid he would enlarge the hole. Within hours, the gurgling would begin again.

Besides the keel leak, there were many leaks in the hull seams. Gerardo tackled these too, but without much success. Breaking out of his isolation, he crossed the length of the boat and asked Juan for help. Caulking boats in dry dock had been Juan's specialty.

"You're the expert," Gerardo said. "Show me the secret."

It was early morning and Juan lay in his corner of the icebox, complaining of diarrhea, which they all had. "I can't show you anything," Juan muttered, and turned over, facing away from the light entering through the hatch. "I'm not throwing myself in the water."

"You're the one who knows this stuff—I don't. I'm just doing what I can."

The older man grumbled that he wasn't budging for Gerardo or anybody.

"Juan, I need your help."

"Go help yourself. You got us into this mess."

Gerardo looked up from his kneeling position on the deck. They were all resting below with Juan. Since the wind was steady and the tiller and sail were tied to one position, bailing was the only required work. But no one was bailing. Gerardo had already finished more than his four hours, and they all made vague excuses for not starting. Peering into the hole, he pleaded one more time.

"Leave me alone," Juan said.

"Do you want the boat to sink?"

Juan didn't answer. He lay in a curl by himself on one side of the cubicle.

Pastor was also by himself, and Jorge and Joel were stretched out belly-to-back in the remaining space.

"I don't understand you guys," Gerardo said softly, then added angrily, "Listen to me!"

Pastor looked up at the heavy-bearded face above him. "What is it, Comrade Fidel?"

"All of you!"

The others squirmed into listening positions.

"I don't care what you think of me, but I'm tired of being your slave. Why should I kill myself working for you guys? All you do is drag your asses around up here to get water or to piss. Why should I bail for you? What are you doing? Nothing. You just want to sleep. All right then, go ahead, sleep."

Gerardo turned away in disgust.

"Finally," a voice muttered from the icebox, "a little peace."

A while later Joel and Jorge, who were called "the married couple" because they slept side by side, began a familiar squabble: "Move your knee." "Again?" "It's in my back." "It is not." "It is." "Is that better?" "A little . . . but watch the elbow." "Let's just turn around . . ."

Another voice interrupted the bickering. "Will you two settle down? It's bad enough having Black Dog up there giving us speeches."

Gerardo slapped the deck and glared at the four cramped figures. "All right," he said, "if you don't want to bail, then I won't bail. We'll all sleep."

"But I can't do it anymore," someone said. "I'm sick."

"Sick, tired, thirsty—everybody's got an excuse."

"My stomach hurts."

"Your stomach hurts, Joel is tired, Jorge feels weak—"

"I *am* weak."

"Okay, then we all die together because this boat's going down. You won't bail, I won't bail. You want to die, I die. It's your decision."

Gerardo slowly returned to the bow, careful not to bang his head on the boom. Some of the fishing-line stitches holding the blanket pieces together had torn and a corner of the sail was flapping free. He tapped the water barrel; not many gallons remained from the tanker's gift. He thought of trying to spear a fish, but he would first have to take down the sail to stop the boat. No, he would rest awhile and later try to catch himself a meal.

Since February 19, when they ate the last of the rice, eating had become a sporadic, individual matter, each man catching what he could for himself. However, a few times when they spotted turtle, they mustered some sense of common purpose.

Joel crouched on the deck, waiting for the animal to approach so he could gaff it at the neck; after it was lifted over the side, Gerardo killed and butchered it; Jorge washed the meat; Juan cut it into small, similar-sized pieces, and Pastor, master of the Bic, cooked them in seawater. If a female turtle carried eggs—or "tomatoes," as they were called—the men each took an equal number of the nutritious treasures that looked like small Ping-Pong balls.

The system worked well, but they hadn't snared a turtle or something large for four or five days. Now, with despair taking hold, the four in the icebox didn't care much about anything.

As he gazed at the pale-blue horizon, Gerardo listened to the keel leak for a while, then heard someone yelling about Juan's farts and how he had cast an evil spell on all of them. The old man brought bad luck and disaster with him from the beginning. They should never have let him join the crew. Juan Evil Eye, Mister Bad Luck—he was the one at fault. If he hadn't been with them, maybe Gerardo would have pulled up the net that first day when the *norte* started blowing. Maybe they'd be home and safe if Juan had stayed behind. Now, they were lost and adrift. They should have tossed him overboard weeks ago, got rid of a piece of the devil before everything went bad. But it was too late. Whatever curse he put on them worked. They were screwed, finished. The only thing left for them was death: death by sinking, death by drowning. But would they really sink, as Fidel had told them? Were they really sinking now, even as they spoke? Would they drown, gagging and swallowing seawater, not breathing, going down and down until they were dead? Or would the sharks eat them first?

Gerardo watched them climb out of the icebox, a frowning Juan emerging last. The older man straggled to the stern rail where he positioned his bare behind over the side and relieved himself. The four went on speaking in low voices, now and then glaring at Gerardo, who lay on his ledge drowsily picking at a callus on the palm of one hand.

Finally, Pastor left the huddle and climbed down into the bailing well next to the engine. He found the bucket sloshing around in knee-high water. Signaling Gerardo with a toss of his head, he shouted, "Okay, papa—we bail!"

Gerardo, naked except for a tattered pair of short pants, had fallen asleep.

Hours later, Pastor was still bailing while the others were mending the sail, poking wire and threads through blankets and slick patches of vinyl. From the time it was first raised, their triangular, thirty-five-square-foot creation was a mixed blessing. Though small for such a stubby, water-laden craft, it did propel the boat, giving the men a sense of control and direction. But fish wouldn't gather underneath as they would when the sail was down and the boat adrift. Controlled by a line running from the boom to a spot under the awning by the tiller, the sail also needed continual repairs.

Though they sailed on a 120-degree, easterly heading, the current from the north moved against them, counteracting any progress eastward toward the Central American coast. But at least the sky was clear and the sea had settled into a gentle expanse of long, rolling swells. About this time schools of tuna and small groups of dolphins appeared at a distance. And when the sail was down, clusters of feisty rainbow fish and fat, blunt-nosed triggerfish, which they called pigfish, also arrived to nibble at the accumulated scum on the wormy, barnacle-encrusted hull. But though the men were ravenous, they seldom dropped the sail to fish, afraid they would lose hours in a futile effort to spear such small prey. As for fishing with baited hooks, which might have been more fruitful, this required meat they'd much rather eat themselves.

One meal they caught without a hook or spear arrived as a sleek, graceful shape touching down on top of the awning. Like a lot of other seabirds, the brown-and-white booby had been swooping and plunging into the water for fish. With their benign, dopey-looking expressions, boobies are bolder than most seabirds and will fearlessly set down on anything that floats. This particular booby wheeled overhead, circling around, then plopped down on the awning roof.

Jorge, who was bailing toward the middle of the boat, studied the web-footed visitor, waiting to see if it moved closer to the edge. When it did, he quickly scooted into the shade of the awning below the spot where he guessed the booby was. The tallest of the men, he reached up and with one swipe grabbed the bird's short, sturdy legs.

For the rest of the day, long after they had plucked the feathers and cooked and eaten the salty, lean meat, the mood among the five improved. Grumbling ceased, the four tenants of the icebox—now called The Penthouse—stopped castigating Gerardo, and even Juan temporarily ignored his stomach cramps that night to make a lantern. Using a can and a kerosene-soaked rope as a wick, he nursed a flame for almost two hours, finally giving it up as too much bother.

In the dark, without blankets and wet from the spray of waves, the men escaped the chilly evenings by dreaming. But the visions of candies, honey, and pastries—anything sweet and unsalty—inevitably turned into nightmares as soon as they awoke and realized it was all a dream. Unlike Gerardo in his breezy, solitary roost, the Penthouse four found themselves in a damp refuge that stank of rotten fish and body odors and was noisy with men muttering and crying in their sleep. One recurrent nightmare that provoked loud moans of disappointment was about their return to Puntarenas. In the dream, the boat would near the dock, the men would see their families, then the boat would return to sea, leaving behind all hope of reunion.

For the men belowdeck the only real escape was to leave the icebox, despite the biting spray blowing over the stern. It was during one of these fitful, evening escapes, on February 29, that one and then all of the men saw a brilliant light hovering over the water about a half-mile away. It was so bright it even illuminated the boat and the surrounding ocean surface. Although no one could discern a ship, the five scrambled to make a torch to signal for help. They waved and shouted, but the light remained fixed at the same position, a glowing white eye apparently watching and waiting. Finally it came toward them, stopped, then retreated and disappeared for good.

By the beginning of March they were rationing the water by spoonfuls, about one every hour for each man. Without rain, at this rate the water might last them less than a week.

"Don't worry about death," Pastor told Joel. The two were squatting by the rudder, slumped against the tiller; both were eyeing the bubbled compass. "God will take care of that. He's got a moment for everything. Just worry about living."

"I'm trying," Joel said, shaking his head, "but I don't think we can go on much more." Pastor started to object, but Joel continued, tears dripping from his face.

"You know what hurts the most? What hurts is that I have to leave my wife and my daughters . . ."

"And I'm leaving Rita a shack. I promised her I'd fix it up."

Joel turned away, hiding his tears.

"Hey," Pastor said, "that's all right, don't be ashamed."

Later, Joel found a scrap of paper and a ballpoint pen in the zippered bag with his change of clothes and a few other items. Separating himself from the others, he picked up a flat piece of wood, crawled to one corner of the stern, and started writing. For a long while, leaving hardly any margins, he printed his words in tiny, cramped letters, line after line. Now and then he glanced at his companions or gazed at the sky and water before returning to his writing. When he finished, he read it over again, made a few corrections, then folded the paper several times and poked it into a small, empty bottle, tightly screwing on the plastic cap.

March 3—My beloved wife. I want to write you so much that I don't know what to say, only that I feel this great desire to live, which is all that gives me strength. But I don't think I'll resist because God is making it very difficult for me. But what can I do? All I can do is wait and go on suffering. Edith, I love you and my four daughters so much. I know if God gives me a future life I will try to change, even though I know that if I die you won't have bad memories, nor will you tell my daughters that I was bad, since I loved them and gave them all I could. I hope someone will be able to send you this, in case I die, because I feel my strength is ending. Don't stop in your life. Be strong and receive God's decisions because He knows why He does what He does, even though there are times we don't know

Crew of the *Cairo III* gathers on the beach in Puntarenas, Costa Rica, after spending nearly five months adrift in the Pacific. Clockwise: Gerardo Obregón (kneeling), Juan Bolívar, Jorge Hernández, Joel González, and Pastor López. (Peter Serling)

Some of the following photos were made from a televised program that included recreated scenes of the trip. Other photos are of the actual rescue, which was captured on video by a Japanese crewman aboard the *Kinei Maru 128* and later broadcast worldwide on news programs.

A replica of the *Cairo III* before its fateful voyage shows a spare water tank and fishing lines stored on the cabin roof. The four-pronged anchor is propped on the bow, and the net is piled on the stern deck beneath the awning. (Directions International)

Juan fights to stay upright in the tiny cabin during the initial storm. At this time, flooding and serious leaks begin and the men must bail around-the-clock in shifts during the next four months. (Directions International)

Adrift and needing firewood for cooking, the crew tears apart the cabin. (Directions International)

With the cabin torn down, the icebox, or fish hold, now serves as cramped sleeping quarters. (Directions International)

All hands lift a part of the heavy, diesel-powered engine to throw it overboard and lighten the ever-sinking boat. (Directions International)

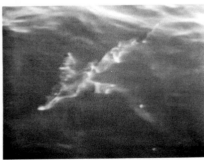

Whether they are in the sea or thrashing about on deck, sharks always pose a threat. (Directions International)

On a rare day of calm seas, Joel waits for a strike so he can yank up his hook and line. (Directions International)

Jorge cleans the catch with seawater. (Directions International)

Under the scrutiny of the others, Jorge slices the fish into equal-size pieces. (Directions International)

Pastor tends the fire in the makeshift stove. (Directions International)

Using a cigarette lighter, Pastor ignites a piece of sponge mattress as kindling for the cooking fire. (Directions International)

In the fight to survive, rainwater becomes more precious than food. (Directions International)

In a televised scene of the actual rescue, a *Cairo* crewman pulls in a line thrown from the Japanese rescue ship. The square, white hatch-cover of the icebox lies on the stern deck, while the boom and lowered sail rest on the plywood-covered fore deck. Two scuppers (water-runoff holes from the deck) appear as dark patches on the hull only inches above the waterline.

Gerardo leaps into the shark-infested sea to grab a life-saver. The jerry-built, wooden rudder can be seen out of the water and set crossways at the stern.

As a Japanese crewman watches, Joel extends a hand to Juan, the last of the Costa Rican survivors to climb aboard the rescue ship.

Edith, with Joel, displays the love note and bottle her husband had planned to toss overboard before losing consciousness. (Peter Serling)

Gerardo and Lidia embrace the day after his return to Costa Rica. (Peter Serling)

第128欣栄丸
岩手県釜石市
KINEI MARU No128

"What surprised me most was that their spirits and energy were so high even after five months of drifting," says Captain Tatsuo Oyama, in the port of Shimizu, Japan. "It's hard to believe they were alive at all." (Akihide Teraoka)

Neighbors and relatives rejoice with Gerardo (in white shirt) and Jorge (tallest) near Puntarenas shortly after their return to Costa Rica. (Peter Serling)

*why. Decide everything slowly, take your time. Help
my mother, take care of my daughters, and tell them I
lost my life in search of a better life, all for them. Tell
them I loved you more than anyone ever will. Here, I
go on, my Edith, waiting for what God has in store for
me. There are two poles, the positive and the negative. I
hope He gives me the positive, which for me would be
to rejoin you again. But if He gives me the opposite,
what can I do? I only know one thing, that if it's
possible to love after life, I will love you. Well, this is
the last I'll write to you, since I see things are so
difficult that I no longer have the illusion nor the strength,
and we're out here two months now and nothing to lift
our spirits has happened. The rainwater that we had is
about used up. We have no food. And all around us,
the same thing—water and more water. God is being
tough on us, but even so, in my last moments of life I
don't deny Him because He knows best. We have suffered so much that I believe that with death He'll actually make us rest. I know that you may never know of
this note, but everything is possible, and if I can't hang
on, I hope God will pardon the life of at least one of
us. That way you can find out when was the very day I
died. And don't spend the rest of your life suffering and
wondering what happened to me. Be courageous and
try to overcome life's hardships, since from the time of
our birth, we know we're going to die sooner or later.
We all have to arrive at that final point. And if God
takes me first, what can I do? I fought till the end and I
did everything that I could to return to you. But at the
end I was defeated. Still, even on the brink of death, a
little flame that won't yet go out remains with me. And
if God is hard in anger, I also know that He is generous
in love—and if not, try to be happy, even if you aren't
by my side, because I will no longer be able to help*

you. If I could, even in death, I would make you all happy. I love Sharon, Rebeca, Emily, and Elke. But God takes them from me. Make them happy, as much as you can. Don't abandon my mother, take care of your mother, try to be serene, and ask God to care for all those who love you, since they are the biggest treasure that you can take with you at your departure. Remember, my love, that I love you, that I loved you, in every moment I was by your side. But before the decisions of God, there's nothing that can be done. I love you, Edith, I love you. Joel Omar.

They were now wandering. They hadn't found rain and they couldn't agree on a fixed course. They discussed *Lifeboat*, an Alfred Hitchcock movie Pastor had seen about a group of people who survived in a lifeboat after their ship had been sunk by a German submarine. The survivors followed the currents and trade winds west.

"They had a plan," Joel said. "What's our plan?"

"Do the same thing—follow the current," someone suggested. "If we keep changing, we'll go nowhere, maybe in circles."

No one objected, although Gerardo hoped this would be their last change of course. So, after they adjusted the sail and rudder, the boat settled on a 330-degree, north-by-northwest heading, which was the easiest, most natural course, given the prevailing wind and current. Their plan, as they put it, was simply "to go wherever God wanted."

Gerardo thought if they went far enough they might wash up on some island—"with lots of food."

"Hawaii," Joel suggested.

Then Pastor spoke, miming a puff on a cigarette. "Just take me to a place where I can get some tobacco."

They tried to imagine where Japan was, how far away

China was, what places were between them and the other side of the Pacific. Nothing specific came to mind except Gerardo's comment that he thought cannibals still lived on some of the islands. He read about it somewhere, maybe *Reader's Digest*, but it had been years since they'd actually eaten anybody.

"Well," Pastor said, only slightly joking, "if things get real bad right here, we might end up eating one of us."

"You're crazy," Juan blurted.

"It's happened before."

"He's right," Gerardo said. "Remember those guys who crashed in the mountains, in South America? That's what they did."

They were quiet for a moment, then Gerardo added, "After eating all that rotten fish, I don't think I'd have trouble eating human flesh. No, sir, no trouble at all."

Despite the course change and a briefly renewed sense of purpose, despair took hold again. They sometimes neglected bailing, mending the sail, repairing the rudder, or keeping a lookout for turtles. They were irritable, argued a lot, and once even fought over a turtle's liver, which they now ate along with the other organs. They were also almost out of drinking water, and to make sure no one took more than his share, Joel was voted to dispense each man's ration.

Gerardo, seeing the others so weak and listless, still worried about sinking but no longer bothered badgering them to bail. Stronger than the others, he figured his body needed less water than theirs.

Then the miracle occurred. It rained. The shower hit them at night during the second week of March. The full moon, which they nicknamed *la linda*—the pretty one— clouded over, the sea grew calm, and the men welcomed the downpour with upturned faces and open mouths. Then they scrambled to collect. They set out a few pots and pails, then two of the men stretched a piece of canvas between them and channeled the runoff into the biggest water tank, which was tied to an awning post. They also made a crude gutter on one side of the roof and trapped water by tilting the boat with their weight.

By the time the shower passed, the five were euphoric. After drinking their fill in the dark, they hugged one another, pounded the deck, and thanked God for hearing their prayers. The rest of the night no one complained about bailing and no one woke up to a nightmare.

Just after dawn, Gerardo nudged Pastor to wake up and take over the bailing. The sky was clear and the sunlight warm. As he returned to his sleeping spot in the bow, he noticed steamy wisps of evaporation rising from the wood pile. A boat, even this boat, smelled cleaner and fresher after a rain than before.

Pastor surfaced from the Penthouse, moved to the bailing hole, and set to work. In monotonous motions, he scooped the water, lifted the pail, and emptied the water so that it ran off the deck through the nearest scupper. Though the sail was up, he could always slow the boat by untying the boom line and letting the sail swing free. Occasionally he looked up at birds gliding, then scanned the water for turtles. Often he saw dolphins and dorados arc out of the water, or glimpsed chunks of Styrofoam and other trash float by.

At first Pastor thought nothing of the tiny, irregular bumps he saw on the southwestern horizon. The sky was clear except for the faraway, dark cluster of rises. It wasn't a ship, so he didn't pay much attention to what the object might be. But gradually, as the boat moved west and closer to the shape on the water, he made out a string of tiny peaks. He climbed up on the awning for a better look, then shouted, "An island!"

In seconds, the others were also squinting and trying to decide if it really was an island.

"Clouds," Gerardo said, still peering. "They're clouds."

"I don't think so," Pastor said. "The little peaks are sharp, see? Clouds are rounded on top."

"The distance makes them that way."

Joel said he couldn't be sure one way or another, but Gerardo probably was right. They were clouds.

After a while they dropped the sail to get a steadier look. Studying the horizon, Jorge said he thought it was an island because the shape didn't change, and a cloud formation would. It also seemed to get bigger and then smaller. "They look like rocks to me. What else could they be?"

"Your imagination," Gerardo said. "It's an illusion, like the man in the desert. He wants something so bad, he'll believe anything, even things that aren't really there."

"How can you be so sure?"

"I've seen them too. It's all in your head."

"But what if it is an island?" Jorge asked.

"It's not."

Someone wondered if they could reach it by sail. Gerardo took another long look. "Clouds. That's no island."

"But what if it were?"

"I told you. It's an illusion . . . a hope."

The discussion was interrupted by the arrival of three small turtles that paddled alongside the hull as if the boat were a giant mother turtle.

About four hours later, after the men had feasted—this time wasting nothing edible—they set sail again. Sated and less desperate, they appeared to forget the island, or the illusion.

Given their approximate, ten-degree-latitude course, the island they saw was probably Clipperton Island, a coral atoll located about sixteen hundred miles west of Costa Rica. The two-square-mile islet was used as a hideaway by John Clipperton, an English mutineer and pirate of the early 1700s. Rocky and uninhabited except for the wild pigs and birds living among a few coconut groves, low scrub and patches of wild tobacco, Clipperton conceivably had enough water and game to support five resourceful castaways.

But the men of the *Cairo* for the moment were no longer hungry, no longer as willing to believe in a convenient island paradise.

After he ate his portion of turtle, Jorge checked the horizon again. The dark, jagged specks were still there, now behind the boat and even smaller. If it were an island, it was too late to go back. The wind and current would be against them and it would soon be dark. Turning away, Jorge shrugged, faced the wind, and delivered a loud belch.

10] SHARKS

Joel tumbled into the sea with a shout. For a moment all was coolness and silence; he floated free and relaxed. Then he opened his eyes, pressed a hand against the glass, and tugged on the mask to create a seal. Ahead, close by, was the boat's shadowy hull with its dangling mat of green-and-brown growth. Kicking his fins, he moved forward. The sea was calm, the sail down, and he and the boat drifted together.

Living by the sea, first in El Salvador, then in Costa Rica, Joel always liked to swim underwater. Whenever he had a chance, he put on his mask and fins, tied lead weights around his waist, and plunged in to explore reefs, rocks, shipwrecks, anything with the lure of the unknown. Later, working on boats, he used his mask and fins to help him untangle lines and nets snagged in the propeller.

Now, as he descended into the shade beneath the hull, he faced only one unknown—sharks. Of all the creatures lurking near the boat, he dreaded them the most. He had caught and killed hundreds of them as a fisherman, knew where to stick the knife to slice the nerve cord to the brain, knew how to bludgeon them into stillness. With quick, impersonal strokes, he had dismembered tons of sharks and never felt threatened or indefensible. But all that carnage was abovewater, where he had his prey at a disadvantage. Here, in the killer's realm, he was abso-

123

lutely certain any fair-sized shark could rip him to shreds in seconds.

Coming up for breath, Joel glimpsed his companions on the stern deck, then went under the boat again. A school of triggerfish parted as he swam among them toward the bow. He poked at the hull with a knife, and smaller fish darted out from the strands of weedy growth attached to the crust of barnacles. Families of little rainbows also appeared, and as he glanced behind and below, he saw a number of big, barracudalike creatures he had tried to catch on the boat but never could. Five or six feet long, they lingered around but had always stayed just out of spear's reach.

Returning to the stern, Joel pulled himself up and over the low, wooden guard rail, removed the mask, and told his crewmates that the barnacles and wood-burrowing shipworms were growing thick on the hull. Earlier someone had told the story of another Costa Rican fishing boat that had been rescued by a freighter after spending three months adrift. The four survivors had asked for their boat to be salvaged, but when it was raised out of the water, the hull disintegrated. It had been so riddled with worm holes that the planking was weakened to the breaking point. The same thing was happening to the *Cairo*'s hull. Besides plugging the seam leaks, they would now have to dive underneath to scrape the hull.

No one discussed who would or wouldn't dive. Like everything else since Gerardo's demotion, they assumed all would participate.

"Let's do it," someone said, and they started making scrapers out of wood and metal scraps left over from the cabin's destruction.

Gerardo inspected the water's surface for any telltale triangular fins, then plunged over the side first. Joel and Jorge followed. Juan hesitated, then lowered himself slowly into the water. Pastor told him, "I'll watch out for the sharks."

Minutes later, Juan surfaced and said he was swallowing water and gagging; he'd stay on the boat and look out for sharks. Much later Jorge joined the two on the stern deck, saying it was hard to scrape and swim at the same time.

Only Joel and Gerardo remained. For hours they jabbed and punched at the rough layer of hard growth, coming up for gulps of air, returning underneath, surfacing, returning, again and again. They were tired and achy, progress was slow, but they worked steadily, occasionally pulling themselves up and resting on deck. Though the water temperature was in the high seventies—warm enough not to chill them—the salt stung their skin, already blistered, chafed, and cut from their hard days and nights on the boat.

At first, when they were in the water, they felt vulnerable. Dangling beneath the boat, they thought the whitish bottoms of their feet would attract sharks. They peered through the swarm of little fish, expecting the worst, waiting for the killer's appearance. Eventually, numb from slashing at the carpet of creatures stuck into and onto the hull, they thought only of finishing. Once Joel tried to catch a triggerfish and they all scattered and disappeared; the fish that would have warned the men of approaching sharks had fled. Now, except for the vague shadows and shapes glimpsed below and in the gloomy distance, the two men were alone.

While Joel and Gerardo were scraping, the others, if they weren't bailing, watched for sharks from the bow and stern. They were used to seeing and sometimes catching hammerheads, black-tips, torpedos, makos, and other medium-sized sharks. And recently, as they moved into the Pacific, they were approached by a much larger white shark. It was about fourteen feet long and looked as lethal as the monster they had all seen in the movie *Jaws*. The big white had bumped the *Cairo*'s hull, scratched itself, and disappeared beneath the boat.

So far today nothing even as large as a turtle had appeared. There were no dolphins, tuna, or dorado. Nothing broke the water, and the only sounds were bird cries and the muffled scraping on the hull.

"That's it," Gerardo gasped as he surfaced for the last time. "Enough."

He pulled himself onto the deck and lay next to an exhausted Joel. For the time being the barnacles were defeated, and although the hull was weakened, disaster was postponed. All that remained were the leaks in the seams, especially under the hull ribs, where the leaks couldn't be plugged from the inside. But Juan, the best caulker of the five, refused to work underwater. "I can't do it," he said in a challenging tone, "and no one can make me do it."

The other four might have overlooked Juan's refusal to work, but something oddly scary occurred. It was not long after the hull scraping had been done and they were again spearing triggerfish and catching dorado and sharks with baited hooks attached to wires. There were still no turtles, but for the first time since they were adrift, they had enough to eat. Joel even caught a tuna by throwing out a hook with a lure made of blue nylon rope threads. They also had about thirty gallons of rainwater stored, or enough to last them two or three weeks. But without turtles as easy prey, the men had to work harder to catch their food; it now demanded hours of concentration, of waiting, poised to strike with the spearlike *chuso* or yank up a line at the slightest tug from below.

Pastor was smoking some meat to cure it, carefully tending the fire, when he saw the thrashing shapes about

.wenty yards away. Three or four black sharks were
churning the water, moving back and forth. Suddenly
they charged the boat. With a thud, they rammed their
snouts into the side of the boat, looped around, and
bashed the boat again. In a frenzy of motion, they hit
and scraped the boat repeatedly, charging and flinging
themselves at the hull.

Then they stopped. No one could explain why the
sharks had rushed the boat, but the men now felt more
vulnerable than before the attack. If just one plank had
been loosened or punctured, the flooding could have
been disastrous.

After the strange assault, Gerardo went into a frenzy
of his own, plugging and replugging the seam leaks. With
a hammer, screwdriver, and pieces of cloth, sponge, and
rope, he scoured the hull from the inside, stuffing the
tiniest leaks. Then, with someone standing lookout for
sharks, ready to pull him out, he hung over the side in
the old sea-anchor tire, filling the seams that were abovewater.

Gerardo needed Juan's help to get at the difficult
outside spots, but the expert caulker again refused.
Gerardo and the others cursed the old man for his stubbornness, saying he was worthless, evil, a danger to them
all. Juan gradually stopped his fish-catching duties and
remained curled in his icebox niche. He emerged only to
bail or scrounge some food after a catch was made. Or
he complained of headaches and stomachaches. Joel,
who had some medicines, gave the grumbling figure aspi-
rin and antacid pills. Afterward, Juan said he felt better,
but he stayed in the Penthouse.

In the late afternoon, the sharks attacked again, only
this time in greater numbers. The onslaught was brief but
terrifying, and the men half-expected them to hurl their
bodies onto the deck, ripping off an arm or two in the

process. Someone joked that they should throw Juan overboard and solve two problems at one time: the sharks would get fed and go away, and Juan would get rid of his headaches.

Gerardo:

Juan is one of a kind. I respected him because of his age, because he'd been around and knew a lot. But you couldn't make him share what he knew. He had to want to share it. I've never met another man like him. He worked only when he felt like it, not when you told him to or you needed his help. He could have shown me how to fill in the seams, but he didn't. You just couldn't ask him for anything because he'd get mad right away. He was oversensitive, as if something else were always bothering him. Maybe he did it to get even with us for who knows what. Or maybe he was always that way, I don't know.

Most people like being with other people. Not Juan. I remember we used to stop in little ports, and as soon as we got off the boat, he'd walk away from the rest of us, just go off and be by himself. Always by himself. That's probably why he got that evil-eye reputation. It's hard to like someone who's so sour and wants to be alone all the time. I stayed alone in the bow, but that was different, that was temporary.

So we started calling him names, like Your Ancientness and Old Evil One. Mostly the other guys did this because they were in the Penthouse with him. But when they came out, he would stay below. The only thing he did was bail. He knew that was the one thing he had to do. I told him if he stayed down there, he was going to die of hunger. It didn't matter; he wouldn't come up.

Jorge:

We'd tease him a lot and he'd beg us to leave him alone. We'd talk about food, and that would really make him mad. But he couldn't do anything about it. Where could he go? He was trapped. If we were outside, all he could do was hide in the icebox.

We all had our lazy periods, but we'd come out of them. Juan would keep on being lazy. He'd stay in his hole, watching us like a buzzard. We'd spend the whole day trying to catch a few pigfish, or Joel would finally hook a shark. We'd cut it up, Pastor would make the stew, and then, of course, that's when Juan would come up looking for some little piece to eat.

We told him he'd have to stop being so lazy. But he played dumb and pretended he wasn't doing anything wrong. So we started rationing his food, giving him just enough to get by but never enough to be satisfied. We wanted to train him to start working again. We gave him a little bit of whatever we caught. He'd swallow it right away and then watch us eat like pigs. We felt sorry for him, but he had to learn.

Pastor:

Juan knew the law—you don't work, you don't eat.

Joel:

I think he was naturally lazy and only worked when he was bored. He helped us out when things got monotonous. But you couldn't count on him for anything. Now and then he'd think of something really clever, but I don't think he did things for us as a group. He'd do it for himself because he was bored and was looking for something to do.

We'd be looking out for turtles, or pulling up the sail, or doing something with the rudder, and Juan would be sleeping. I told Jorge that the old man was faking, that he just wanted to last longer than us, that he was resting and eating, saving himself so he'd live longer. "All right," I said. "Let's not starve him; let's just give him very little portions, enough to teach him a lesson."

Juan tried to escape by staying in the icebox. He even stopped eating for a week. We'd yell at him and tell him if he kept up his tricks he was going to die. Finally he started correcting himself. Something must have made sense to him because little by little he joined us and started working and eating and not hiding so much. He still had his weird moments—we all did—but at least he was doing what the majority ordered.

He had no choice but to cooperate. If he wanted to live, he had to do what we said.

"How many squares are on one side of a checkerboard?" Gerardo asked early one afternoon.

"Eight," Jorge answered, intrigued.

"Good," Gerardo said, kneeling on the deck with a knife and ticking off spaces for eight little squares. "Let's make a board."

A game might distract them from their thoughts for a while. The sail was up, and since no one was fishing, Gerardo figured he could carve a board in the deck.

"What about the checkers?" Jorge asked, and someone suggested making them out of pieces of a plastic jug. While Gerardo carved the sixty-four-square outline, the others cut the plastic pieces and blackened half of them with charcoal. Alternate squares were deepened and also blackened.

Everyone but Juan was eager to play. He watched the others at a distance, muttering and sometimes dozing. Joel and Jorge, the two sports fanatics and the most competitive of the five, played until sunset, winning and losing about equally.

"What's the point?" Juan asked them when they were finishing their last game.

"You play, that's all," Joel answered, moving a piece. "Does there have to be a reason? I like games."

"It's silly."

"Old man, you're the one who's silly. All you do is sit there and complain. Now you're complaining about us playing checkers."

"I'm not complaining."

"Then let's talk about real games. Your son plays soccer. And he's good, right?"

Juan brightened and nodded.

"Is he silly?"

"No, but he's young. He can do those things."

"And you can't?"

"I'm past my time."

"Do you play any games . . . anything?"

"I watch my son play."

"You watch anything else?"

"No."

Jorge spoke. "How about baseball?"

"Never, that's for all you Nicas."

Jorge, whose family was from Nicaragua, looked up from the board. "What's that supposed to mean?"

Juan turned away, frowning.

"Well?"

"Too many Nicas," Juan grumbled. "Send them all back."

Jorge was about to respond when Joel, the Salvadoran immigrant, interrupted. Glaring and pointing a finger at Juan, he said, "You're the one who should get out of the country, you old illiterate."

"Nicas, Salvadorans, all of you ought to—"

"Hey, hey," Gerardo shouted from the bow. "You guys should hear yourselves. We're out here in the middle of the ocean and you're trying to kick each other out of the country. What country? The only country you've got is this boat. That's it. So what do you say we get along?"

"Look who's talking," Juan said. "It's because of you that— "

"Enough of that stuff," Joel said.

"You want to forget it? It's his fault we're out here."

"Juan, whatever happened before, already happened. Let's talk about now. Gerardo's right—we've got to get along. All this stuff about I'm right and you're wrong, or you're right and I'm wrong—so what? What difference does it make? Just look around you. We're nowhere. Old man, this is nowhere."

They attempted to play checkers the next day, but lost interest and quit. Nobody again discussed the status of Nicaraguans or Salvadorans in Costa Rica, and Joel said nothing more about Juan's illiteracy. The old sailor began cooperating, fishing and cutting up pieces for Pastor to cook. But still, something was gnawing at him, something that made him almost destroy one of their two remaining knives.

One morning while scaling and cutting a small triggerfish, Juan couldn't filet it properly. Cursing the knife and mumbling that it was dull and useless, he began hitting the blade against the sharpening stone.

Gerardo rushed over and told him to take it easy. "You're going to break it," he said, trying to take the knife away. "That's not how you sharpen it." But Juan was gripped by anger and frustration.

Then Joel came from behind and grabbed the knife. "Imbecile," he screamed, raising it above Juan. "You ruin everything. How can we keep anything if you destroy it?

You stupid old man. Just because you're bitter, you don't have to drag us down with you."

Juan stared wild-eyed at the knife. "But there's no way to cut this damn fish."

"Watch, so you'll know," Gerardo said, taking the knife and quickly slicing the flesh from the spine. "The knife is fine, the blade doesn't need sharpening. It's you, you're the problem."

Joel continued shouting at Juan, saying he had no right to destroy what belonged to all of them.

"All right, enough—leave him alone," Gerardo said. "I think he knows what he did."

"I doubt it," Joel said. "We lose our knives, and then, what?"

Juan returned to cutting the fish, but the rest of the day he kept to himself, glowering, silent and pensive.

Juan:

I lost interest. Just dragging my ass. Lazy. No energy. I'd wake up feeling lousy, didn't care about anything. We were going to die anyway, so why should I do anything?

So I stayed in the icebox and waited for my time to bail. They'd yell at me and call me names. Always call me names. Old man, grandpa, evil eye. If I did something wrong, like the time I hit the knife, they'd jump all over me, screaming I was stupid and no good. They were like sharks, all over me, always picking on me. They blamed me for everything. They said I was bad luck, and they'd be better off if they threw me into the ocean.

Then they punished me. They started giving me just a little meat. Even if they had a lot, they wouldn't give me much. They'd fill their own stomachs, and all I could do was watch. I'd go back to the icebox. I stayed there for weeks, licking my wounds, I suppose. I even stopped eating for a while. See, out there the mind works overtime. All you do is think. Day and night, you think and think. You can't sleep when you're hungry, so you just lie there and think.

I thought of my children a lot. I had a picture of my son, of Santos. I was the only one with a picture of anybody, and I'd look at his picture. I even showed it to the others. But that was hard because it hurt and I wanted to cry. Out there I couldn't go home. I'd open my eyes and I knew I was trapped.

That was the horrible part. I couldn't go anywhere, couldn't escape. Just stuck on that damn boat with the four of them acting like sharks. See, I'm not a sociable person. I never have been. I go where I want to go, do what I want to do. That's me. But being out there, I couldn't do anything and it was making me a little crazy. I didn't know if I was going to eat, and I couldn't stand that. But what could I do? There was nothing I could do. By the time they punished me, I was pretty far gone. But the punishment was just. I had to help. I couldn't stop working just because I felt bad. We were all miserable.

Before the last rain, Joel and Gerardo tacked a canvas strip on one side of the awning to make a wider gutter, but everyone could see it wouldn't do. The wind blew a lot of water over the gutter, and much of what was trapped missed running into the tank below. The water they had collected was almost used up, and now it hurt to remember what they lost. Someone mentioned boiling seawater and collecting the evaporation, but that would mean burning a lot more wood. They agreed the awning and the half-dozen containers they had were the best means of catching rainwater, but they needed a more efficient system if they weren't to die of thirst.

The main problem was the wind, which except for a few calm periods had blown steadily ever since the *norte* hit them.

"I've got an idea," Juan said after studying the awning and poking around the wood pile. "We need a bigger gutter. We also need something to channel the water into the tank." The men listened attentively, aware that he was a clever man when he put his mind to solving a problem. Juan's solution required the addition of three items: a plank of wood, a short piece of a hose, and a funnel. He took the hose from the engine, and he made a funnel by cutting the bottom off one of their last plastic jugs.

As he hammered and cut, the others mostly watched. When he finished, the gutter was higher and wider, the funnel was nailed to the lower end, and the hose ran into the tank from the funnel.

"Now pray for rain," Juan said.

Pastor clapped him on the back. "If it works, you get the next turtle liver."

"But we haven't caught a turtle in weeks."

"Ah, correction—*if* we catch a turtle."

The others nodded, and Juan sat back and waited for the big test.

Several days later, around the end of March, it rained, the new system was a success, and Juan proudly accepted compliments. His spirits were lifted even more when a few days later Jorge gaffed a turtle. But as the lanky young man was lifting it up, at the last moment it slipped away.

Juan, as hungry or more so than the others, watched dumbfounded as his meal—especially the liver—paddled off and disappeared in the swells. While the others cursed

Jorge for his ineptness, Juan moved off by himself to scan the water's surface. For a while he pictured turtles, then he started thinking about sharks and how similar they are to people when they get mad and hungry.

11] THE WHALE

April began harshly. The wind that struck in the night churned up waves almost as high as the *norte*'s giant breakers. With its sail down, the *Cairo* pitched and bucked almost as wildly as before. One moment the boat was heaved up, the next moment shoved down. But no one panicked, as the open, leaky craft somehow remained upright and afloat, like a bobbing, half-filled bottle.

At first the men were afraid the waves would sweep them overboard, so they stayed belowdeck—Gerardo under the bow, the others in the icebox. Then the water began to swamp the uncovered, middle section, and one by one they crawled over the deck and found receptacles.

Throughout the night, they bailed blindly. Soaked, chilled, and with nothing to see in the darkness, they worked by touch, clinging to anything solid only when they felt the boat dropping into the curl of a wave. Again and again, they braced themselves, waiting for either tons of water to smash down on them, or for the boat to ride up the face of the wave to the crest. Most of the time the *Cairo* climbed to the top.

Whoever bailed in the boat's lowest part sometimes stood waist-deep in the water, but the men believed the boat would never really founder. The *norte* had challenged them with bigger waves and they had survived. So they would do it again, this time by fighting back with steady, mechanical efficiency. They wouldn't stop until the water in the engine compartment was down to a safe level.

As long as the boat wasn't flooded to the point of sinking, it remained remarkably stable in the water. With the weight of the water and a six-hundred-pound engine serving as ballast, the *Cairo* kept its hull pointed into the water and showed no signs of capsizing.

By daybreak, under a dark, overcast sky, they could see the gale was passing. Gradually the wind and the wave heights dropped, and the sea became tame enough to raise the sail. When the sun broke through, they knew they had triumphed.

To the five adrift, the April storm became a turning point. Until then, they saw each problem, each period of thirst or hunger, as the final crisis. Every mishap, every loss, pushed them to disaster. If someone lost a turtle, it wasn't viewed as a mere accident—it was practically their collective death sentence. If one of them drank or ate more than the others, it was a crime and the culprit was scolded or punished and made to feel like a criminal, an outcast. Whatever the incident, it was seen as one more nail hammered into their coffin.

Then the storm hit. This time they had no cabin protection, the leaks were worse, and they were growing weaker. But they set to work anyway, grimly determined at least to die on their feet. When they emerged alive, they began to realize survival was possible. God still pulled the strings, but as long as the boat didn't sink, they had a chance. "If we die, we die fighting," Pastor said. Joel, off by himself, prayed they would have the strength to face whatever lay ahead.

Not long after the storm passed, Gerardo sharpened a knife on the whetstone, faced the sunlight shimmering off the water, and cut the first handful of hair from his head. "Filth," he announced, slicing off another clump and flinging the black curly wisps over the side. The others watched him start at the top and work his way back to the neck.

"How about the beard?" someone asked, and Gerardo said, no, he would need a razor to cut that close. Besides, it was his scalp that itched, not his face. Recently he imagined he was developing a crust of half-healed sores beneath his tangle of hair. Every day his head was exposed to the tropical sun, and every day his scalp accumulated the residue of sweat, seawater, fish scales, bits of flesh, and squirted blood. He squirmed at the idea that his scalp might make him sick, that the sloughed-off scum of the boat's rotting wood, of their bodies, of everything that he touched, might somehow infect him with disease.

After cutting his hair, he rinsed himself with potfuls of seawater. Without soap, he was as clean as he could get. If he were going to survive, he had to stay healthy. He would not become like Juan, whose depressions led him to neglect his body. Joel had poured iodine on Juan's open scalp sores, which helped, but he shouldn't have had sores in the first place. Gerardo promised himself he would bathe more often, scrub his scalp, brush his teeth, and eat all he possibly could.

One after another, the Penthouse four picked up the knife and cut their hair. None had Gerardo's heavy facial growth, but they all had mustaches, which they left alone. They also bathed, careful not to douse themselves with seawater that might contain jellyfish. It happened once before to Juan and the excruciating stings lasted for hours.

The sudden compulsion to trim and clean themselves not only signaled the start of a new, more positive attitude toward their plight, but it also probably helped

them avoid serious skin problems. Sea survivors invariably report they were plagued by sunburns, sores, wounds,
boils, and abscesses. But the *Cairo* five were free of the
usual skin ailments, suffering mostly cuts and nicks from
the handling of fish, turtles, and sharks. Besides their
frequent bucket dousings, the rain occasionally rinsed
salt from their bodies, the awning provided them with
shade, and they used turtle fat or antiseptic ointment
from Joel's little medical cache to treat themselves. They
also used the remaining diesel and kerosene as liniments
for stiff muscles and sore joints.

Apart from their initial bouts with diarrhea and weight
loss, so far the men were relatively healthy. They had
endured periods of thirst, hunger, and despair, and had
emerged if not stronger, then more determined to stay
alive. Gerardo's mania to remain disease-free and to
keep the boat seaworthy now rubbed off on the others.
They began to tackle survival as a group effort, with
specific duties for each man and an understanding that
everything should be done for the common good.

Their roles in catching prey and preparing meals continued as fixed as ever: Joel caught, Gerardo butchered,
Jorge cleaned, Juan sliced, and Pastor cooked. They also
kept to the four-hour bailing shifts with the five-gallon
plastic pail. But if someone with bailing duty was busy at
a crucial task—fishing, mending the sail, or repairing the
rudder—whoever was free took over the bailing.

Gerardo:
You couldn't just think of yourself. You had to think of
the five. It was five or none. But I could see it was hard
for them. I was by myself in the bow, usually quiet, just
observing, so I didn't get into it with them. But they used
to fight and argue, and I'd tell them not to. I told them we
were brothers, and like brothers, we were tied together.

The devil isn't some man with horns and a tail. The devil is other people, bad people. None of us was bad, not really. I never felt that. So why shouldn't we get along and work together?

Our biggest enemy was laziness, idleness. Out there it was easy not to work. But lying around is when you started thinking and dreaming. When the dreams took over, you were lost and had no control. It happened to me many times. Once I dreamed I ate two loaves of bread and drank a soda. Then I ate some mangoes and other fruit. Well, I woke up. I was mad at myself for letting the dream take over. Thinking of home and food—that's dangerous. You can't do that because it's a fantasy. If you're all the time thinking of that, just lying around, dreaming, and doing nothing, then you're useless.

I had to forget the past. And the best way to do that was by staying busy. It was the only way to forget. The hardest times were at night. That's when you're alone with your thoughts. But in my case, I was next to where the cooking was done, so I'd help Pastor. With all that smoke, I couldn't sleep anyway, and I thought I might as well make myself useful.

Pastor turned out to be a real worker. A lot of times he'd stay up most of the night cooking and taking care of the fire. Then he'd be up the first thing in the morning asking what there was to do. He ate more than his share, but that was his payment for cooking our food. He also took care of the Bic. That was important. The Bic was the most important thing on the boat.

"Whoever doesn't like me eating the best parts, then fine, they can cook. You don't like me eating double my share? Okay, you stay up all night, you watch the fire, you prepare the meat. See if you can do it." Pastor glared at Juan, who was complaining that the cook ate more liver than anyone else.

"You eat all you want and whatever you want," Juan said. "I don't think that's right."

"That's my privilege."

"I count out the pieces, and I try to be fair, but I can't watch you all the time."

"You don't have to, old man, because right here before your eyes I'll eat everything I can get my hands on. It's no secret, I'm a glutton."

"You're disgusting."

"If you want my job, then you're welcome to it."

Juan glanced around at the others. "You know I can't work the lighter. You're the cook. I just thought you were eating too much."

"I am."

The other men supported Pastor's position. They knew the painstaking work it took to keep them all fed. He had to cut slivers of wood for kindling, hack up the bigger pieces with a machete, light a bit of sponge or cloth with as few strokes of the Bic wheel as possible, get the wood to burn, then finally spend hours cooking forty or fifty finger-size portions of flesh, which was about what an average, ninety-pound turtle would yield. He was also an expert at frying the meat in turtle fat, which became their favorite seasoning. And he had the patience to try curing meat with smoke, a procedure that demanded even more attention than "cooking" a meal in warm-to-hot water.

No one challenged Pastor further. He was keeper and master of the white plastic lighter; as long as it didn't run out of fuel, he was the wizard of their tiny flame. The men saw the Bic as their link to land, to home, to a civilized life that included fire and cooked food. They also felt this way about their two watches, which were never changed from Costa Rican time.

But the Bic was imbued with something more. The

lighter took on the importance of a spiritual, life-giving relic, and Pastor, its sole user and guardian, was practically given the respect of a priest. So, when he stumbled and dropped the Bic into the water flooding the hold, the others held their reproaches. Stunned, they watched in silence as Pastor jumped after it, felt around, and fished it out. Muttering to himself, he carefully dried and blew on the lighting mechanism. Then he spun the wheel with his thumb. When the flame appeared, everyone cheered. They would not have to eat raw meat.

Not that raw meat would have harmed them. Most survivors of long periods at sea report eating nothing but raw or sun-dried meat. But because the *Cairo* crew had a stove and wood to burn for cooking meals, they ate with gusto and not only boosted their protein consumption but also their morale. Fire also gave them warmth and even a slight sense of triumph over an otherwise bleak and watery world.

By now they were eating everything they could swallow except what was bitter or foul-tasting, such as bile or the contents of intestines. They threw anything edible into the general stew—organs, muscles, bones, membranes, gristle—and probably for this reason they suffered no serious vitamin or mineral deficiencies. Their vitamin C, for example, probably came mostly from the eyes, brain, and pancreas of the triggerfish, one of their staple foods. Every time the men sucked and swallowed one of these organs where C is concentrated, most likely they helped heal their cuts and prevented the onset of scurvy, that gum-bleeding, seaman's scourge of another time.

Some days the men speared forty or fifty of the eight- and nine-inch triggerfish. They also began catching more turtles, which now appeared in greater numbers than ever before. They caught, almost exclusively, Olive Ridley turtles, the world's most numerous species of sea turtle. So, with more available, catching them became a routine matter. The men hid or remained still until one approached. Then usually Joel, the best at this, sprang up to grab a flipper and pull the animal aboard. The crew's only regret was that the boat had moved so far from land that they no longer caught females with their treasures of "tomatoes," or eggs.

As for dorados, they could be speared or hooked with a line. Usually chasing flying fish, the blue-and-golden-yellow dorado often hid in the shade under the boat. Gerardo, trying to skewer one of these visitors with a small harpoon he made, once scraped the clublike head of a three-footer. He escaped and from then on kept his distance. For some reason, Scarface, as they named him, never left them.

Another regular visitor that first appeared in April was a booby that stayed around for weeks. The large white bird repeatedly approached the men to stare at whatever they were doing. Jorge finally caught the goofy-looking bird and banded one leg before letting go. The booby disappeared for days, then returned from the north. He did this a number of times, and the men were convinced Jorge's bird was flying to land and back. They wondered if they should follow it. But since the wind and current were from the west, it would be difficult or impossible for the boat to tack north. Meanwhile, whenever the booby visited, he was treated as a sort of mascot.

About this time, other birds they had never seen before began to appear. Large, gull-like, big-winged creatures, they seldom flapped their wings like land birds; instead, they soared, glided, and rode the air currents. They also saw flocks of smaller white birds flying north. These had black patches over their eyes, parakeetlike beaks, and long, reddish, pencil-thin tails. Probably red-tailed tropic birds, they too reminded the men that land might be just over the northern horizon.

But the boat was moving farther and farther west. Sunsets were getting later, and from their watches, set to Costa Rican time, they could tell they had crossed at least two time zones. Instead of the sun setting around six, it disappeared after eight.

Gerardo:

We were advancing. Thinking about how far west we'd gone made us feel better. Sometimes when the moon was out, I'd sit by myself looking out over the water and wonder what country we'd get to. We all thought about countries and islands, because now it looked like we weren't going to die so fast.

The birds would remind us of land. A lot of them seemed to be going north. Sometimes they'd stop on the boat and stay awhile. That's what happened with Jorge's white bird. It lived with us. Never really bothered us much. Gave us something to look at or talk about. Most of the time it stayed on the awning. We had enough to eat, so we didn't think of killing it.

One night, just before four in the morning, I was bailing. The moon was out and I could see the bird. The guys were asleep, so it was nice having the company. I remember checking the time. It was about five minutes to four. I kept bailing, feeling the wind, and listening to the water slap the side of the boat. Then I looked at my watch again and it was four. I looked at the bird again, but I could barely see him. He was lying down. I stopped bailing, went over, and picked him up. He was dead, poor thing.

Maybe it was old age or maybe he got sick from something. Anyway, we plucked him, cut him in pieces, and fried him in turtle fat. The meat was dry and had very little juice to it, but that bird was a good change from what we usually ate.

*   *   *

"You think about women?" Joel asked. It was dark and the Penthouse four were huddled in the icebox.

"My wife, yeah," Pastor answered.

"I mean sex? Do any of you—"

"Ah-ha! I knew it," Pastor said, and mentioned the "married couple"—Joel and Jorge. "You guys need to be alone?"

"I'm serious," Joel said. "I don't feel a thing. I wondered if I was the only one like this."

"Don't worry, I'm inert, zero."

They all admitted they hadn't thought of sex or had sexual desires since right after the first storm. Given their circumstances, their lack of interest was probably normal, but it still worried them. As a test, they decided to talk about women—all kinds of women. They described every female feature they could envision, every desirable aspect of a woman's body. They recalled movie stars and beauty queens, remembered girlfriends and prostitutes, told true stories and invented others. But none of it worked. The four remained unmoved. As far as arousal was concerned, they could have been describing the water or the sky.

Like most of their discussions, this one helped them forget the tedium of hours spent awake in the dark. The sex talk also provided the men with a nickname for Jorge, whom they had been calling Lazylegs because of his unsteady moves. From now on, he was Boom-Boom, the name of a popular dance hall and bar in his hometown, a place where he often met girls. The new tag stuck, although Jorge—once a hard-punching boxer as a teenager—wished his companions were referring to one of his heroes, the American lightweight Boom-Boom Mancini.

On another night, when sports was the topic in the Penthouse, Jorge recalled how he lost his last bout. "They stopped the fight because my nose was bleeding."

"Boom-Boom," Joel said, "tell the truth. It was a knockout, wasn't it?"

"No! I had the fight won. Just a little blood and they stopped it."

Joel uttered a doubtful-sounding grunt.

"I swear I had the guy beat."

"Who cares?" Juan interjected. "Change the subject or shut up."

Sports talk always irritated Juan, but he was imprisoned, forced to stay in the icebox, especially after sunset. So he had to listen to endless, repetitive arguments between Joel and Jorge, the two jocks.

Tonight, after discussing the relative merits of Mike Tyson and Larry Holmes, they tried to decide, once and for all, which sport was the king of sports—baseball or soccer? Not just in Costa Rica or Central America, but in the world. Joel said soccer, Jorge said baseball. The shouting escalated until Juan and Pastor begged them to stop. Finally, Gerardo stopped bailing and leaned over the open hatch. "Hey, boys," he called down, "remember where you are. It's not going to matter one way or another." The two quieted down but not until they finished one more looping discussion about professional wrestlers.

Gerardo's reminder was reinforced a few days later when they sighted something very large and dark coming toward them under the water. Then it emerged, shooting a fountain of water into the air. The men had seen whales and whale spouts before, but always in the distance. Now, they watched stupefied as the huge black shape approached them head-on.

Given the boat's steady westerly movement, the *Cairo* was about midway between the Galapagos Islands and Hawaii. This was the same area where a rogue sperm whale rammed and sank the whaling ship *Essex* in 1820, providing Herman Melville the ending for *Moby Dick*.

The whale that was now racing toward the *Cairo* wasn't white, but it was probably a sperm whale as big as the eighty-foot leviathan that stove in the *Essex*.

Gerardo grabbed his harpoon, which wasn't more than a broom handle with a barbed spike tied on the end.

"What's that going to do?" Joel asked.

"Just in case."

"In case what? Look at the size of that thing."

Pushing a wave of foamy water ahead of itself, the whale steered straight for the center of the boat. Certain they were about to be hit and sunk, the five men braced themselves for the collision. Gerardo, dropping the harpoon, positioned himself to jump clear when the boat broke up.

But at the last instant, the whale dived, barely missing the hull with its immense fluke. After the whorl of water settled, the men stayed still, quiet, waiting for the inevitable. They were still sure their fragile boat would be destroyed. One slap of the tail, even a bump from that giant square head, and the hull planking would snap.

They waited about five minutes, then peeked over the side when they felt movement beneath the boat. The whale appeared to be nibbling at the growth on the hull. With nothing they could do to encourage it to leave, the men waited, helpless, terrified. Then the whale surfaced alongside the boat. Ten feet away, it rose with a loud, steamy blast from its blowhole. The spray blew over them, but the whale remained, an enormous creature with a single observant eye fixed on the little boat and its five frozen figures.

"My God," Gerardo said, "it's like a piece of land."

For twenty minutes or so the whale seemed to court the boat, diving under it, swimming around it, sidling up to it. What was the creature up to, circling, curious, playful? Though the men were afraid, they controlled their fear. After a long while they began to accept the whale's massive presence as a visitor with apparently no evil intent.

After it left, Gerardo examined the harpoon, thinking at most it might have tickled the whale. The others laughed and Joel said something about not fighting what you can't change. Just then, as if to punctuate Joel's comment, Scarface, their dorado companion, leapt high out of the water, its glinting blue shape airborne for a moment. Then it came down with a splash and was gone.

Gerardo:

There were a lot of things we had to accept out there, not just whales. Like each other, and that wasn't always easy. If you didn't like somebody's smell, or if someone was in your spot—you know, where you liked to sit and put your ass over the side—well, if you didn't like it, what could you do about it? You couldn't tell him to leave and go shit somewhere else, could you? What good would that do? No point in that. So you ignored it and went about your business. After a while, we didn't care anyway. We had no shame. Nobody turned around or anything. You just did what you felt like doing. Who cared about looks and good manners? Nobody thought about that. You just accepted things—bad smells, bad habits, bad luck, everything. Like Joel said, you didn't fight what you couldn't change.

So when the whale showed up, sure, we were scared, but we had to accept the whole thing. I had this harpoon, and I was thinking I'd hurt it or scare it away. But when it got right next to us, I realized how impossible, how stupid that would be. It was so big—just the tail was bigger than the boat.

What could we do? We waited to see what would happen. And it went away. No problem.

12] THE NET

By April, public interest in the *Cairo*'s fate had died. Although the Puntarenas coast guard still broadcast a daily call for information on the boat's whereabouts, most people considered the vessel sunk and its crew drowned. In the port's bars and plazas, in its churches and living rooms, at parties and all the other places where people met, if the *Cairo III* was mentioned, it was usually in tandem with the *Dragón 2*, the city's other, more recent missing boat.

Only among the *Cairo* crew's families was there talk of hope. Edith and her mother continued their visits to the local spiritist, who was always encouraging, and Lidia attended Masses to bolster her faith. Other relatives dreamed the men were still alive, or they expected news from Panama or Nicaragua that the crew had been found and was safe. Some even believed another country had imprisoned the men as suspected spies or guerrillas.

But as the days and weeks passed, Edith and Lidia found themselves increasingly isolated in their belief that Gerardo and Joel were still alive. Treated by neighbors and friends as widows, they were urged to resign themselves to their husbands' disappearance. Months had gone by without a sign or piece of evidence to the contrary. There had been no sightings and nothing had washed ashore. The storm had caught them, the sea had swal-

150

lowed them—they weren't coming back. And if the women believed they were, then they were to be pitied as heart-sick wives, blind to the obvious.

Depressed and with little appetite for food, they lost weight, neglected their appearance, and wandered about the streets like sleepwalkers. Occasionally, they earned money by selling raffle tickets or washing and mending clothes, and relatives helped by giving them food and loans and taking care of the children.

Every day Edith called the coast-guard station, and every day the answer was the same: no sign of the *Cairo*. She also made repeated calls to Victor Monge at the Foreign Relations Ministry in San José, and though he had nothing positive to report, he encouraged her not to lose hope. He was especially interested in what Edith said about the spiritist and never discounted the possibility of the man's telepathic powers.

About this time, Edith was organizing a trip to the capital for a meeting with the public security minister, Hernán Garrón. As the man over the coast-guard vice-minister, he was one rung higher in the ladder of command, only one removed from the president himself. She requested an audience with Garrón and was waiting for a response. If he refused to see her and the rest of the crew's relatives, she vowed to carry her fight to the presidential palace to make one final plea for action.

But many people believed her efforts to push the government into action were futile: too much time had passed and the government was not interested in searching for five poor fishermen. None of this could persuade her to give up badgering the authorities. As long as her hope remained strong, she would not stop.

One afternoon in late April, Edith answered the phone, listened a moment to the caller, then started screaming. Joel's mother, who had recently arrived from El Salvador, rushed into the room to see her daughter-in-law crying and hysterical.

"What happened?" she asked, alarmed and afraid she might hear news of her son's death.

"The net, they found the net," Edith said, sobbing.

"What net?"

"The *Cairo*'s net."

"That's all?"

"And a buoy with the *Cairo*'s name on it . . . and a hand . . ."

Edith hurried to her bedroom, where she spent the rest of the day alone either screaming or crying. "Leave me alone," she shouted if anyone tried to talk to her or console her.

Later, the details became clear. A fishing boat had found the net floating about fourteen miles off the coast south of where the *Cairo* was thought to have been fishing. The report of a human hand found tangled in the net was a rumor started by someone's imagination when the net was stretched out and examined by coast-guard officials. The entire net was brought into port intact, its thick anchoring line apparently torn from the boat.

Most people who heard of the discovery were now convinced that the *Cairo* had sunk and that that was the end of the matter. But after Edith regained her composure and puzzled over the find, she concluded the net's existence proved the boat was still afloat.

"It's a good sign," she told Lidia and Pastor's wife, Rita. "If it had sunk, the net would be attached. But it's not because it broke. So the boat and the men are still out there, waiting to be rescued."

"The government wanted a clue. Well, now they've got one," Lidia said. "Let's see what they do with it."

The visitors from Puntarenas entered the imposing, high-ceilinged waiting room of the ministry about two in the afternoon. Their appointment was for two-thirty. The group included Edith, Lidia, Rita, Pastor's mother, Hilda, the boat's owner, Carlos Rohmán, and several friends of the crew. They had come to the capital by bus, hoping that with more people present at the audience, the minister would feel more obliged to help them.

Of all of them, Edith looked the most tense. She was weary of polite answers and mock concern from receptionists and guards, secretaries and clerks, men in uniforms and bureaucrats in dark suits. How could they know what she was going through? The days and weeks of never knowing, the nights alone in bed thinking of Joel, imagining his suffering, wondering if he and the others had water and food, thinking of the island Pandora, praying for their return, begging God to save her man. Would the minister understand? Would he help them?

By three o'clock, everyone was restless and growing impatient. The minister's secretary said the minister had been delayed and was running a little behind schedule. After an hour more of waiting, they reminded the secretary of their appointment, but she could only shake her head and shrug in sympathy. To Edith, the big room's atmosphere felt cold and impersonal. Most of the time the group was ignored; they were promised coffee but none was served, and when they were noticed, the glances were practically hostile, as if the assemblage of fretting visitors were a band of provincial troublemakers.

Finally, around four-thirty, the tall, wide doors to Hernán Garrón's office opened and the *Cairo* group was shown in. A balding, portly man, the minister was older than his vice-minister, and Edith thought he had the measured movements and bearing of an important man. As Rohmán and the wives stated their case, Garrón listened attentively, then gave vague assurances that the government would do what it could to continue the search for the men. However, he suggested the women consider the possibility that there was nothing more to do but wait.

"How about the net?" Edith said. "Isn't that proof that they're out there waiting to be rescued?"

"Not necessarily."

"Can you send out planes?"

"We'll see, it may be possible."

"And the big patrol boat? It still hasn't gone out."

"I've been told it's being repaired."

"Well, why don't they fix it? What does it take? What's going on?"

Garrón was becoming annoyed at the young woman's insistence. He knew she was distressed, and he tried steering the discussion in other directions. But Edith was adamant. Finally, the minister glanced at his watch and said he was late for other commitments. The half-hour meeting had raced by, and Edith thought they had barely begun. Frustrated and angry, she clenched her teeth as he rose, forced a smile, and went around shaking hands, wishing them much luck in their long vigil. Before she slipped out the door, Edith noticed the old man had the same expression of pity that neighbors back home had whenever they greeted her.

On the ride home, Edith and Lidia discussed taking the next step: asking for an audience with the president, Oscar Arias. Surely, such a reasonable, sensitive man, a family man, a man who had won a Nobel peace prize—surely he would help them, he would give the orders to start a real search.

The next day Edith called the presidential palace to ask for an audience with Oscar Arias. She emphasized the urgency of her request and was told by a lower official that they shouldn't have any problems being granted a meeting. After several days and more calls, she and the others were given an appointment date and told to present themselves at the outer gate of the presidential grounds.

This time Edith appeared accompanied only by Pastor's wife, Rita, and his mother, Hilda. They stood in line with other people, and when they reached the gatehouse, the young guard looked at the three anxious faces and asked them what they wanted.

"We have an appointment to see the president," Edith told him.

The guard nodded. "I don't think so."

"Look in your book there," Edith said, motioning impatiently toward the gatehouse interior. "Or call inside. You'll see."

"I'm sorry, you can't go in," the guard said smiling, amused.

"What's so funny?"

"Nothing, nothing. It's just that—"

"That what?"

"The president's out of the country."

"But we were told—"

"Sorry."

"We've had this appointment for weeks."

"It takes months. Two and a half minimum. I don't know who you've been talking to, but not just anyone can get an audience."

Hilda spoke, lifting her chin, slightly defiant. "We're the women of the *Cairo Three*," she said loudly.

Most of the people in line perked up when they heard the words. The guard thought for a moment, then blurted, "Oh, those guys are dead! Why bother—"

"Why bother," Edith snapped. "That's none of your business! It's not your problem, so you shouldn't stick your nose into it. You don't know anything about it. And what you said is cruel and unjust."

"That's right," someone in the line said.

"Yeah," another added. "How do you know they're dead?"

Soon Edith started crying and the crowd of curious sympathizers continued to scold the perplexed young man.

Later, on their way home, Edith remained silent. She had tried her last recourse and had failed. What was left? What hope was there now? Where or how would she get the strength to go on, day after day, with only her prayers and a spiritist's vision to keep her faith alive?

A pile of letters from Joel arrived postmarked Korea. In Edith's dream, they were spread out on the kitchen table, all with the same stamps. She picked up one envelope, opened it, and found 750 American dollars, with a note from Joel. "This is all the money I have. I'll send you more later. How are the kids? Buy them clothes. I'm okay. Good-bye, Joel."

Lidia listened as Edith told her about the dream. "And that's it?" Lidia asked. "That's all he wrote?"

"That's all. Nothing tender, no Love, Joel. He forgot me."

"You don't know that."

"I know."

"At least he sends you money, even if it *is* a dream."

Edith raised her eyebrows and gave a wan smile. "Hmm, but I can't spend that kind of money."

13] MAY 10

My beloved. Incredibly I'm still alive, since by this date I thought I would have been rescued or dead. But so great is God's power that even from here I can wish you a happy birthday, and my mother a happy Mother's Day. Because up to the tenth of May, I am still alive. And I pray to God you are all well, even though I can't be at your side. But don't ever forget that I love you, because I believe I'm suffering for your pain, not mine. After this May tenth, I don't know how much more life remains for me. I'll await God's decision with courage, since I'm praying with all my will to be reunited with all of you. But if it's not that way, then may His will be done. I pray to God that He take care of you and protect you, that you understand there are things that have to happen sometimes, for better or for worse. With all this time that has passed, with all the suffering, I go on loving you, my daughters, and my mother, since even near death you are everything to me. I love you without limits. I can't accept reality, but that's the way the end is. I don't regret what I had in life, because it was the best. A great woman, beautiful children, and a great mother. I love you all, and if God doesn't reunite us someday, I ask that He make you happy. I love you, Edith, I love you. Joel Omar González Rivera.

*   *   *

About three weeks after the whale encounter Joel wrote Edith for the second time. He sat on the stern deck in a corner, apart from the others, and pulled the scrap of paper out of the little brown bottle. He wrote on the flat top of the raised side bordering the stern and started his message with the date. For him it was a special day—Edith's twenty-sixth birthday and Mother's Day in El Salvador, where his mother lived. As he wrote, he only wanted to convey his love toward the two women and his daughters, and to say he was resigned but not defeated. There were no details about his condition, no mention of the crew, no information about winds and currents, food and water, bailing or sailing. No incidents or descriptions. Nothing but his own yearning, his own prayer.

He wanted to spare Edith the true picture of his last days. If his note were ever to reach her and the girls and his mother, even years from now, he wanted them to remember him as a loving husband, father, and son, not as the wretched, castaway creature he had become.

Joel stared at his companions. They were pathetic reflections of himself. Like him, they went through each day naked and uncaring about anything except food, water, and staying afloat. Darkened from the sun, ribs showing, their hair in tangles, they looked like primitives, desperate men whose appearance alone would frighten the meanest of dogs. Gerardo, with his Fidel beard, still showed muscles on his arms. Pastor and Jorge looked scrawny and wild, and Juan appeared fragile, sickly.

After almost four months at sea, Joel was sure everyone at home had given up on the *Cairo*'s return. Without clues, without bodies washed ashore, who knows what visions Edith had of his end? Eaten by sharks? Drowned? Starved to death? She had no way of knowing they were still alive. If there had been a search, it was probably a short one and done close to the coast. And if a ship had reported them, had anything been done about it? He remembered the Chinese tanker and the angry captain. Was that their last chance to be rescued? Or was it the mysterious, hovering light that had come and gone in the night? Or maybe it was the island, if there had been an island.

Joel looked out over the water. It was calmer today than yesterday, and they were sailing with a good breeze, trolling a few lines with their rope-thread blue lures. Now and then they caught something this way, but most of the time they dropped the sail and waited for the hull—which had again become a hanging garden of algae, barnacles, crabs, and other tiny creatures—to attract fish and turtles.

There were no rain clouds, just high, wispy streaks, so high they never seemed to move. The last rain squall had come and gone around the time of the full moon, a few weeks after the whale scare. The moon—*la linda*, the pretty one, the delicate white one surrounded by a gauzy, misty halo—always seemed to bring rain when they needed it most. They didn't collect much—about thirty gallons—but if they rationed it carefully, they would have a month's store of water, or more than three cups a day, if rationing were exact, which it never was. Somebody always drank more than his share. The day's heat, combined with the loss of perspiration from all their energy spent bailing and fishing, made their bodies cry out for more water. So as long as they had it in the tank, why not drink it now? They would collect more when the next shower hit. *La linda*, pretty as ever, wouldn't forget them.

But if it didn't rain, Joel thought, then what? Who would die first? Old Juan? Jorge? They were the weakest, especially Juan. He may have changed his earlier, no-work attitude, but he could still lapse into moods when he wouldn't eat, coming out of the icebox only to bail. Even then he would grumble about having to do his shift. But he knew the penalty for not bailing, he knew they wouldn't hesitate in throwing him overboard. Everyone had talked about the penalty, and there was never any doubt—they were absolutely serious about this. Bailing was all that protected them from the sharks. Anyone who wouldn't bail, who refused to help the majority, would be eliminated.

As the leaks grew worse, the bailing became more urgent, even when the waves were down. Joel felt no one would risk death by skipping a bailing shift. They were more likely to die from thirst and hunger than by being shoved into the water for not working. They all agreed if they were too weak to fish or catch turtles and had nothing to eat, then the body of the first man to die would be placed on the awning roof and treated as a source of food. Raw or cooked, it wouldn't matter how the flesh was eaten.

Joel remembered how he ate the rotten dorado and shark during their first hungry month. A burning ache in his empty stomach drove him to cut the meat into small, thin pieces, then one by one he swallowed them without taking a breath. Now, if he had to swallow bits of a dead man's leg or his liver, he would simply do it the same way.

Joel watched Gerardo lowering himself over the side and wondered where he got the energy to hang suspended on the tire, half of him in the water, hour after hour, hammering and wedging bits of cloth and rope between the hull planks. Of all of them, he was the strongest, the most determined not to sink. He never spoke about being reduced from his captain's position, but from the way he went about scraping the hull or filling in the seams, Gerardo, in his quiet, decisive way, seemed to have taken the initiative again. He avoided discussion and just slipped over the side and started working. It was his own solitary way of doing things. Ever since Joel had known him, Gerardo was always taking on the jobs no one else wanted. The man was a beast for work.

Joel remembered the time Gerardo tried to rouse him from a morning stupor by ridiculing his past. They had all been talking about the different jobs they had held in life. Gerardo, noticing that Joel lately had been acting sluggish and more than usually depressed, flatly told him, "You never had to kill yourself working. You don't know what it's like. You had it easy. Mommy and Daddy took care of you, sent you to school, bought you good clothes, taught you manners, made you a gentleman. But what did you know about real work? When you were in school, I was digging trenches in the field or picking coffee in the mountains. When you were playing with the girls, I was cutting sugarcane. I had to work, you never did. No one ever made you work. Fishing—you call fishing work? Man, fishing is easy time. Lots to eat, plenty of sun, and a nice view. There's time to sleep and time to lay around and scratch yourself. Work? Come on, Joel, fishing's a vacation. You want the real thing, go work the earth, go sweat under the sun with all the flies and bugs and snakes, with all that mud and filth and your hands cut and bleeding every day. That's the kind of work that kills. Not fishing. Fishing is just roaming around, taking it easy."

Joel wasn't offended because what Gerardo said was true. His own life had been easier. But then few people could match Gerardo in early hardship. He was just a kid when his mother died in his arms. And his father had already left him and the other kids, so Gerardo had to take his place. That was when he was eleven or twelve and they lived in the *campo*. So how could he go to school?

Of course, he was right. Joel had lived an easier life, probably easier than all of them. Jorge on the farm, Juan with odd jobs and all those years fishing from a little sailboat, and Pastor with his clamming—they all lived hard lives. Pastor even spent a year in prison for hitting a cop. It was really a labor camp. Hard work, he said, but at least he knew when he was getting out. Not like here on the boat, where nothing was sure.

Joel glared at Pastor, now bailing. Usually the small man with the quick smile was talking. He talked about anything, on and on, silly things or serious things. His family, his clams, his little boat, his friends, his time in prison, movies, the bible, anything. He was restless, nervous, had to talk. At two in the afternoon or two in the morning, it didn't matter. Once he started, they couldn't stop him. All they could do was tell him to shut up or turn away and escape to the bow. But even without an audience, Pastor delivered his monologues, speaking to himself or to anyone who would listen, real or imaginary. "I feel dead if I don't talk," he said, and explained that God gave him a tongue for a purpose. "I won't stop using it until I die."

Even when he fell into the water for the second time, he wouldn't stop talking. Joel remembered the waves were up that day. Pastor was on the bow and had spotted a ship on the horizon. As if he could be heard at that distance, he started shouting and waving the tattered orange life jacket. Then he lost his balance and toppled over with a shriek. When he bobbed up about ten yards from the boat, he was muttering about not losing the ship. The boat was drifting away with each swell that hit, so he let go of the life jacket and with fast, frenzied strokes swam toward the stern.

"How about those sharks?" he said as they pulled him up. "I guess they don't like skinny, dry meat."

The ship had continued on over the horizon; the men had stopped their puny effort at making smoke, and Pastor, unusually silent, had moved to the bow. He was staring glumly at the tiny, dark plume disappearing in the distance. Later he told the others how easy it would be to leave, to step off into the sea and end it all.

"You're crazy," someone had said.

"Maybe, but I think about it. I think sometimes God has forgotten us or He's mad at us. What have we done that's so horrible? Why so much punishment? He must like to see people tortured. Out here like five little fools, jumping up at every ship that passes. And the ships will never stop, even if they do see us. We're nobodies. Look at us—we're not worth it. So I was thinking, Why not save God the trouble of killing us slowly, why not do it ourselves? Over the side, splash!"

"Hey, man, shut up."

"I mean, this would be one way out. But then I thought maybe God was punishing us, or pushing us, to see how much of this shit we could take. And here we are, months later—we're still taking it. But why? I mean, why, dammit, why?"

"Whoa! That's enough, *basta!*"

As usual, Pastor continued—until he concluded that God had given them life to live, not throw away. No one had the right to throw it away.

Joel remembered Pastor afterward announcing they were about to run out of wood to burn. He was smiling, almost cheerful. They had already finished burning the wood that had been the forward part of the cabin, and all that remained was kindling.

So Joel took it upon himself to scavenge for more. With a few makeshift tools he pried away every plank and block of wood that was unnecessary in keeping the boat together. Mostly he recovered pieces from the hull's outside trim and from the inside bracing between the U-shaped ribs. Pastor told him it was enough to last two or three more weeks—"or as long as God keeps filling the Bic with lighter fluid."

That was weeks ago, and Joel now noticed how careful Pastor was in removing the ashes from the opening at the bottom of the little hibachi. Then he cleaned the tiny wheel grooves in the lighter head with the sharpened point of a wire. Clever, Joel was thinking. He was a good man to have on the boat, even if he did have a mouth he couldn't control.

It was late, just after sunset, and a brilliant, reddish-orange glow filled the western sky. Joel reread the note. This day would probably be his last May tenth. For him it would be Edith's last birthday and his mom's last Mother's Day. Edith was still young, still beautiful, and it hurt him to think he was leaving her with four girls to raise. How would she do it without him? Her parents would help her, but sooner or later, painful as the idea was, he admitted she would have to marry. That was only practical, logical. Still, it hurt to imagine Edith with another man, the girls with another father.

Joel cried openly, and the others left him alone. He would never see his daughters again, never see them grow, finish school, marry, have children, his grandchildren. He'd made plans, promises. He was only starting, and all he wanted was a chance to make something of himself. Somehow, if he ever escaped from this, if by some miracle he returned, he promised himself to be a better husband, a better father.

"Hey," a voice said, "it's your shift."

Startled, Joel blinked the sunset back into focus, nodded, and raised himself from his corner spot. After storing the bottle in his athletic bag, which he also used as a pillow, he left the Penthouse and retrieved the plastic bailer that was floating next to the engine. Methodically he began to scoop the water, lift it up, and spill it onto the deck. Out of the corner of his eyes he could see Gerardo looking in his direction. It was about the only direction Gerardo could look, since to be comfortable he had to lay with his head tucked under the bow deck and facing the stern.

Gerardo was probably thinking about the leak around the keel screw. It had grown larger, yet he was afraid to pack it any tighter with cloth because the surrounding wood was so rotten. If he applied too much pressure, the hole could pop open completely, creating a breach too large to patch. The same was true of the wider, hull-seam leaks. Gerardo guessed they had about three, maybe four weeks left before the leaks gave way and the water gushed in faster than they could bail it out.

Joel wanted none of this in his note, although he thought he might add a few lines about the causes of their disaster. As he bailed, he listened to Juan hum a melody from the thirties or forties. Even though he hadn't eaten since yesterday and was probably feeling weak, Juan was in a surprisingly upbeat mood. Joel figured the pulled tooth had something to do with it. Juan had been complaining about a loose front tooth for weeks, and finally Pastor convinced him to let him yank it out with a piece of string. The tooth came out on the first try, leaving Juan grinning with relief.

For a long while Joel bailed in silence, trying—as Gerardo urged—to concentrate on the present, trying to forget the past. So he concentrated on his duties, on the bailing, on the condition of the boat, on the high seas that always seemed to hit them every ten days, on better ways to wrestle the turtles, on morale, on the sharks, on the whale, on Scarface, on the sunsets and the moons and on all those things he didn't write in the note because he wanted Edith to remember only that he died with his thoughts by her side. He tried to forget, tried to feel only the water around his ankles. This should be the only thing that mattered—fighting the leaks.

But on this day, especially today, Joel couldn't dwell only on the present. His mind kept returning home. Toward the end of his shift he was softly singing, over and over, a Julio Iglesias ballad about living and dying. The song had haunted him for months, and though he forgot parts, he remembered the essentials and pronounced them as he would a prayer before meals: people are born and people die, people laugh and people cry, but life goes on, life is the same.

At the end of his shift, Joel glanced at the luminescent watch dial, then pulled himself up onto the deck. The breeze felt warm on his skin. He was tired and hungry. He yawned and stretched his arms outward, then found the cup to scoop some drinking water out of the tank. In the darkness he caught several flashes of light in the water and wondered if their fellow traveler, Scarface, was staying with them. He yawned again, gazing up at an infinity of stars.

Holding on to an awning post, Joel faced the ocean and urinated. He was sleepy, still looking up and vaguely hoping to see a shooting star, when he heard Gerardo's voice.

"Joel! You're pissing on a turtle!"

Joel looked down just as the big shell dipped beneath the surface and disappeared into the dark.

Both men waited for the turtle to return, but it never did.

14] LAST ENTRY

"Boom-Boom."

"Yeah?"

"How can you be a baseball expert and you don't go to baseball games?"

Jorge was carving a cross out of a small block of wood. Without pausing, he answered Joel, "I didn't say I was an expert. I said my dad was the expert."

"All right, you're not the expert," Joel said. He was sharpening a fishhook point. "So, then, how can you tell me baseball is the king of sports?"

"It just is."

"But how would you know?"

"My dad told me."

"But where's the proof?"

"Where's *your* proof? How can you prove soccer is the king of sports?"

"I don't have to. They play soccer everywhere."

"Not everywhere."

"Well, in more countries than they play baseball."

"You don't know that."

"I do."

"Sure."

"So where do they play baseball? Nicaragua and the United States. Two countries."

"Japan."

"Three."

Joel and Jorge would have continued arguing, but they were interrupted by Juan's excited "Turtles ahead!" cry.

With its sail down, the boat was drifting toward a patch of dark-green humps bobbing in the easy rise and fall of the swells. Some of the turtles were copulating, the males locked onto the backs of the females. Others paddled around separately, their heads craning upward, eyeballing the strange object in their midst.

In the next ten minutes or so, Joel flipped onto the deck two small turtles and a larger one whose shell was about two feet wide. One after another Gerardo quickly slaughtered the animals, removing the pale-yellow bottom plates, catching the blood in a container, then cutting out the entrails, organs, and muscles. Jorge rinsed out the intestines and filled them with coagulating blood to make sausages.

Unlike their wasteful use of turtles in earlier months, they now ate or used most of their catch except the heavy shells, which weren't even needed as water collectors. They split the bones and sucked out the marrow; they stripped the coarse, leathery skin from the flippers to scrub their pots with, and they made bracelets and necklaces from the bones, or scrapers from the toothless, beaklike mouths. Gerardo even carved a pair of earrings for his daughter from a turtle's claws. He cut and cleaned them, then looped strings through holes made in each one. The earrings dangled from the strings meant to pass through his daughter's tiny pierced ears.

Whenever they entered an area with a lot of turtles, the men caught only enough to last them two days. With such an abundance of these creatures lately, there was no need to catch more. Besides, the meat would start to rot after two days. So, after they caught the three turtles on the day Joel and Jorge interrupted their ongoing, king-of-sports debate, they hauled up their shabby sail and caught the wind.

They had no way of knowing their speed, but Juan, the sailor, figured they were moving fast because they were almost keeping up with the school of tuna racing along with them in the distance.

Pastor had warmed the pieces of turtle meat, and they had eaten until they were full. Gerardo was bailing and Joel kept repeating a pop-song refrain about there being no place like Hawaii. They were used to one another singing certain favorite songs over and over, but Joel's monotonous Hawaii line began to grate.

"Change the station, will you?" someone said.

Joel stopped without a word, but when Gerardo started singing a rock song with the words, "I'll never return," Joel cut in with his own version of a song with the line, "I will return."

Soon they all joined Joel, and for a while the mood among the men was almost cheerful.

A few days later the glow began to die. It was mid-May and several critical changes in their lives were about to occur. The changes were easily predicted: they would soon run out of wood, and if it didn't rain in the next week, they would also finish the drinking water. Also, there was the continual leak crisis, with the boat increasingly taking in more seawater and consequently riding lower in the swells.

The men decided to dismantle the six-hundred-pound engine and dump it overboard. Gerardo, a self-taught boat engine mechanic, unbolted various parts with several wrenches, much of the time groping with his arms and hands underwater. With tremendous efforts by all of the men, they lifted the main block of the Volvo Penta engine, inching it up onto the deck, raising it slowly to the top of the side, then releasing it. The dirty hunk of gray metal hit the water with a big splash, followed by other, smaller parts they had removed. The boat was now hundreds of pounds lighter and they also had more room below for bailing.

As for the coming water shortage, there was little they could do beyond imposing stricter rationing. For the time being they would keep it to three cups a day for each of them, but they all knew that without rain, they would soon be drinking two and eventually one cup a day. More than a lack of food, they dreaded thirst the most.

They were better prepared mentally for the inevitable exhaustion of the wood. Pastor had been a magician with the Bic, treating his tiny flame-maker as if it were a priceless object, nurturing the countless fires, getting the most out of each splinter and plank of wood. He did what he could. But all along they knew that cooked, fried, and smoked meat had been a luxury. Now they would have to eat everything raw. At first the idea had been revolting, but the more they thought about it, the easier it was to imagine chewing and swallowing everything from turtle brains to shark eyes.

About the time they dumped the engine, Joel exploded in anger one afternoon when they had dropped sail to fish awhile. Jorge was trying to hook a dorado that appeared to be hiding from a shark in the weedy hull growth underneath. Instead of the dorado biting, the shark tangled several lines and bit off a number of baited hooks until only one hook was left. Joel screamed at Jorge for being inept, stupid, and a danger to all of them. By losing hooks, he was limiting them to catching fish with only the spearlike *chuso*, which was more difficult.

"That leaves us with one good hook," Joel said. The other men also looked angry and disgusted.

"I'm sorry."

"What good does that do?"

"Hey, it's done. I can't bring them back."

"Imbecile! Don't try to do things you can't do. We needed those hooks."

Jorge, squatting near the icebox, seemed to shrink even further from Joel's verbal onslaught. He was silent—until they caught a small shark they called a "cheese shark" because its meat tasted like cheese. When Gerardo slit the stomach open, out spilled the tangled lines and hooks. A villain no longer, Jorge eagerly offered to help cut up the meat.

On May 16 they caught a large mako shark. After Joel and Gerardo pulled it out of the water with the gaff, struggling to flip it over onto the deck, it appeared to be about nine or ten feet long. It was still alive, twisting and arching its great gray body, whipping its tail against the awning posts, thumping its head and jaws on the deck. The men raised their weapons—metal pipes and a few pieces of wood—and began clubbing the shark on the head and spine. After the initial beating, which went on for ten minutes or so, Gerardo moved close and plunged a knife into the rear part of the head. His target was the brain, and he had to be careful not to break the blade against bone when making the thrust. The shark quivered, whipping its tail again, and Gerardo backed away.

The men spent almost an hour subduing the mako, alternately clubbing it and stabbing it. Finally the twitching stopped, Gerardo sliced off the dorsal fin, and rolled it over on its back. Blood had turned the white belly pink. To sever the head, he cut in short, sawing motions ahead of the gills, then tugged at the torpedolike snout and slack jaws to free it all from the body. "Okay, done," he said, and tossed the head onto the hatch cover of the icebox.

Whenever sharks were caught, one of Jorge's duties

was to scrape away the skin and flesh from the long snouts. This would be used as bait, while the organs and flesh from the inside of the skull were set aside to eat. After they finally killed the mako, Jorge felt a sense of relief and triumph, but he was tired and distracted with thoughts about the coming feast. They were used to catching four- and five-foot sharks, easily subdued on deck. But today's shark was two or three times that size, and his arms ached from all the bashing and clubbing.

He was catching his breath when he noticed Gerardo was cramped for room to do the butchering. "I'll get this out of your way," Jorge said, reaching for the bloodied head. Normally he picked up shark heads from the bottom and the severed end to avoid touching the teeth. But this time, the big mouth was open and the top rows of jagged teeth presented a convenient, if dangerously sharp handle. So he casually reached under the top of the snout, inserting his hand, and lifted up.

The jaws snapped shut. For an instant the head dangled from Jorge's hand.

With a howl he jerked his hand back, tearing bone-deep gashes in his thumb and two fingers. Screaming, he bent over in agony, his wounds dripping blood between his legs. The others laughed and someone asked why he had stuck his hand in a shark's jaws. Jorge's mind was too blurred with pain to answer, but later—after they had tossed him a piece of cloth to wrap his hand in—he explained he thought the shark was dead.

"It was," Gerardo said, "but the jaws weren't."

"A nerve," Joel suggested, "probably a nerve still alive."

Jorge's knees wouldn't stop shaking, then his whole body started shivering.

Pastor finished the flesh-scraping of the skull, then

rubbed Jorge's legs with the last of the diesel they had saved in a plastic jug.

"Dumb," Jorge blurted.

"Just don't do it again," Pastor said, massaging a trembling knee. "We're almost out of diesel."

"I didn't do it on purpose."

"Relax."

"It hurts," Jorge whined. He was sitting on the deck, his long legs stretched out, rocking back and forth. "Who would have thought that could have happened?"

"Believe it or not."

"What?"

"The TV program." Pastor finished the massage and tapped Jorge's knee. "They'd believe you."

Jorge moaned and drew up his legs. "Thanks," he said, and closed his eyes.

Not long after his jaws accident, Jorge woke up in the night screaming for his father. This was followed a few nights later by Juan's fit of hysteria. In both instances the others in the Penthouse had to soothe and calm down the screamers, talking them back to reality. Jorge simply wanted to embrace his father, and in the nightmare he could never get close enough to the tall, gaunt figure. But Juan's outburst culminated months of frustration and brooding about death.

Of all of them, Juan was the most convinced that they would die, that they had no chance to survive. He had been forced to cooperate with the others, but many times he wanted to die quickly instead of being slowly tortured to death by hunger, thirst, and an overwhelming sense of entrapment. The night he lost control, he slammed his head against the icebox wall, babbling and muttering about not going on.

In the morning, he looked less worried and gloomy,

sociable for a change. Usually a recluse when he wasn't needed, he even volunteered advice and treatment for Joel's stiff neck. "It was the wind and the water," he explained. "If you want a cure, cover it, wrap it up nice and warm."

Joel was surprised and pleased by the old man's sudden concern for someone other than himself. Maybe the bad-luck spell had worn off. He was about to thank him for the advice when Pastor announced there was no more wood to burn. "From now on, boys, we eat raw."

And they did, cautiously at first and in very small bites, but soon their hunger forced them to eat larger mouthfuls of whatever they caught. Gradually they seemed to lose their taste and there was a sameness about everything, except turtle liver, their favorite meat. And lately there were always plenty of turtles about.

But if it didn't rain soon, even an abundance of floating meals within easy reach would not replace their drinking water. Without much discussion, they agreed to reduce the daily ration to two cups a day. This arrangement lasted only a few days. They realized that with two or three gallons left in the tank, if they drank a combined total of ten cups a day—or more than half a gallon—the supply would last only another three or four days. So they decided, despite some grumbling, to cut the ration to one cup and thereby extend the supply by a few days.

May 26 was Jorge's twenty-seventh birthday and they celebrated with a last extra sip beyond their normal one-cup ration from the water tank.

Survival experts generally agree that the average person needs at least one pint, or two cups, a day to survive adrift in tropical waters. Anything less, and severe dehydration begins, followed by an often irresistible urge to drink seawater. If this is done to any great extent, delirium, then unconsciousness, then death occur. The men of the *Cairo III* knew that drinking seawater could be fatal. But when they decided to cut their ration to one cup a day, they didn't expect their minds to be so quickly affected.

The nightmares and arguments increased. The tempers were shorter, the shouting louder. Some of the men drank their ration all at once, others drank half in the morning and half at night. Everyone watched everyone, and if Joel, the elected water dispenser, spilled any on the deck, the others shouted all kinds of angry accusations at him.

In the Penthouse, the four bickered about one another's body smells and noises, about hogging space, about suspected slights and insults. By himself at night, Gerardo started hearing faint engine sounds of faraway ships. Yet, when he scooted out of his niche to have a look, there were never any lights to be seen. Searching the horizon all around, he thought his mind was working tricks to confuse him, to take his attention away from the here and now.

About three days after the one-cup rationing began, Gerardo had a vivid dream about an island. Unlike the nightmare visions of the others, his dream was a pleasurable experience. In it, the men were welcomed by a crowd of beautiful, friendly people who pulled them onto a long, wide beach dotted with more turtles than they could ever eat.

The boat was pulled onto the powdery white sand, and soon their hosts gave them spoons, plastic plates piled with rice and sugar, and various kinds of cool, refreshing drinks.

This dream was followed by another in which the *Cairo* was about to arrive in Puntarenas but was asked to help tow in another boat. But the other crew was starving, begging for something to eat. Gerardo said that he had no food to give them and that they were starving themselves, that they were so hungry they could eat wood. By the time he woke and the dream ended, neither boat had returned to port.

In the morning Pastor noticed that Gerardo was standing on the bow ranting at the wind with his fists, accusing an invisible enemy in the sky of withholding the clouds, of stopping the rain, of trying to kill him and the others. He cursed the wind, the sky, cursed the cowardly rain for hiding itself.

Pastor had never seen Gerardo, normally the most reserved and controlled of the five, taken over by such a fit of wild shouting and mumbling. Pastor was bailing at the time and was irritated by the incessant raging at the wind. He thought of saying something to quiet the man, but he knew it wouldn't do any good. Whatever desperation he felt, Gerardo had to let it out. The man never cried, as he and Joel did, nor did he scream in the night like Juan and Jorge. He just stayed in his spot, staring at the sky, hardly ever talking. Now he was on the edge, wasting his energies shouting at the wind.

Suddenly Gerardo moved toward the stern, picked up a metal scraper, and said the hull needed to be cleaned again. With the sea calm and the sail down, he would start immediately. He reminded them to keep a lookout for sharks, then plunged into the water, his naked body disappearing after the splash. Three of the Penthouse four took up positions around the boat to watch for anything suspicious breaking the surface.

Throughout the afternoon Gerardo repeatedly surfaced for breath. Finally, he pulled himself onto the stern. Exhausted, he lay back, his chest heaving. After a while, he sat up. Someone handed him the cup with a little water at the bottom and said, "That's the last of it."

"What?"

"There's no more."

Gerardo, his body now crusting with salty smudges, tilted his head back and put the cup to his lips. He swallowed once, then set the cup down. "Thanks."

Pastor continued bailing, Jorge and Juan returned to the Penthouse, and Joel added a last entry to the note to his wife. After he finished, he poked the scrap of paper into the bottle, then inserted some Costa Rican paper currency. It was only a few dollars' worth of money, but he thought it would be enough for postage for anyone sending the note to his wife. He also tied his high-school ring to the top of the bottle, just below the cap. Then he put it all in his bag, ready for the time when he would throw it into the ocean.

Shipwreck Causes:
We were working normally when a strong wind began to hit us. So we tried to find the coast, but the engine was very small, not much capacity, and our diesel tank was also very small. We soon ran out of fuel, and we couldn't get back to the coast. The radio didn't work, so we couldn't communicate. We tried, but we couldn't do it. The wind made us its prisoners, but even so, we managed to hang on until the first part of June. But in vain. Please, whoever finds this note, I ask them to send it to the following address . . .

15] THIRST

Using a pencil, Joel wrote his, his wife's, and his daughters' names on the inside of the hull, then added the date—June 1, 1988.

"Why are you doing that?" Juan asked, looking on. "You're only making it harder on yourself."

"You're right."

"Remembering them, thinking of them."

"But if I don't do this, how will they know how long we were out here?"

Juan shrugged and continued bailing. His movements were slow and deliberate as he bent down, scooped the water, raised the bailer, and tilted it over the side. His face was gaunt and his dark skin stretched tightly over his ribs and hip bones.

Joel searched the horizon for clouds while the other men were dozing or staring blankly at the water. It was already midmorning, and the heat was making him sweat. He asked Juan for the bailing bucket, dipped it into the sea, then poured the water over his head and shoulders. He thought of spitting out the water that dribbled into his mouth but swallowed it instead. The sudden jolt of liquid on his skin and in his mouth felt good, and the breeze soothed and cooled his wet body. Joel raised his arms to catch the soft westerly wind, then doused himself again with seawater, this time keeping his mouth closed.

178

With the rudder broken and unusable, they had dropped the sail, swinging the boom around so that it pointed out over the water from the bow. No one felt like fixing the rudder because they figured it didn't matter where they waited for rain. They could try sailing farther west, but the sky looked as clear in that direction as it did where the boat was now. It had been about a month since the last shower hit, and lately even the full moon, *la linda*, showed no signs of bringing them rain.

No one felt much like fishing either. Turtles, dorado, triggerfish, sharks, and tuna were plentiful, but the men's interest in eating appeared to have dropped as their thirst increased. Joel and Jorge speared a few triggerfish, and rather than eat the slices of raw flesh, they sucked on the meat, squeezing out what little moisture they could.

Throughout the morning and long past noon, they waited, feeling the breeze, leaning as the boat rocked and tilted in the swells and white-tipped waves. Dolphins zoomed underneath, surfaced nearby, and uttered a barrage of squeaks.

"Maybe they're trying to speak to us?" someone said.

The smiling gray snouts poked out of the water about twenty yards away.

"Superman," Pastor said. "We need Superman."

Joel corrected him: "Aquaman!"

"Yeah!" Pastor said, brightening for a moment, then calling out, "Aquaman? Where are you?"

For a long while they were silent, glum. Gerardo took over the bailing and Juan returned to the icebox. The heat was oppressive, though not too humid. But without water to drink, the five men felt a fiery suffocation crawling up their chests, around their throats, and over their faces.

After Gerardo finished his shift, instead of returning to the bow he remained in the shade of the awning. He stood clutching a post, staring at the sky and sea, and began to mutter to himself about the wind. He accused the wind of teasing and torturing them, of letting them stay alive so they could suffer slowly. If the wind had no intention of bringing rain, then why should it exist at all? Why not go away? Why bother them?

The other men had heard the previous tirade, only this time Gerardo spoke with an edge of desperation in his voice and eyes. It was the first time they had seen him so agitated, but no one said anything. He would quiet down once he unburdened himself. It was a normal process; they had all gone through it and usually felt better afterward.

But by late afternoon Gerardo continued to harangue the unseen enemy, this time mumbling and muttering his rage while seated on the bow facing the sea.

Finally, Pastor dropped the pail. "You! Listen to me," he shouted at Gerardo.

Gerardo stopped and turned to listen to the small, wizened-faced clam-digger.

"The wind doesn't bother me now," Pastor said. "You know when it bothered me? It bothered me when it should have bothered *you*, when it would have made a difference. At the beginning when we started out, when the *norte* hit us—that's when it should have bothered you. So don't talk to me about wind, Captain. Now it can blow as hard as it wants, as long as it wants . . . Hey, it doesn't matter anymore."

Gerardo was quiet for a moment, then he said he just wanted the wind to bring rain, nothing more.

"We all want that," Pastor said, "but we're not going to get it because we got something else. We got the biggest, cleanest, deepest grave in the world."

Gerardo made no more declarations against the wind. As far as he was concerned, it was a miracle they were still alive or hadn't all gone crazy. He was even surprised he could control his own sense of hopelessness. Pastor was right to get angry. What good would yelling at the wind do?

It was just that for a while he thought they had a chance, that they might survive, after all. He thought they had been through the worst, that nothing could be as bad as the *norte*. They had bailed like madmen and lived. And they went on living, fighting hunger and thirst, taking the cabin apart, making a sail, collecting water, catching fish and turtles, and somehow, always, they managed to stay alive. He thought nothing worse could happen to them, that from now on their only big worry was keeping the boat afloat. And he could do that himself—he didn't need the others. He could scrape the hull and plug the leaks without their help. He didn't mind. He'd make sure they survived.

Now this. How were they going to live without water? They couldn't drink wind. But that's all there was. Wind and wind and wind. And seawater, thousands of miles of seawater. Pastor was right. It would make a clean grave because by the time you hit the bottom, the sharks and other fish would have eaten all your flesh. Nothing would be left but bones.

Dying was probably easy compared to this waiting. This was the hardest part, waiting for the rain that would never come. Without water they would get weaker and weaker until they couldn't move because their bodies were shriveled and dried. When he died, it would be a relief. Close your eyes and nothing else. He wouldn't feel a thing, wouldn't know when it was over because he would be unconscious.

Was it God that was punishing him? Was it all his drinking? Hadn't he promised God he would control himself? But maybe God wasn't satisfied with a promise.

Maybe God wanted to punish him so bad that he'd never forget his promise, or he'd learn a good lesson—like the time he, Gerardo, had punished a man for mocking a smaller, weaker man who only wanted to be left alone. They were members of a crew from years ago, and Gerardo had warned the bully to stop taunting the other man, to pick on someone who could defend himself. "Pick on me," he remembered saying. And then they fought, but not for long because Gerardo's attack had all the quick intensity of an execution. He might have killed the man, but he was pulled away by other crewmen.

He thought of the beating as a punishment, not a torture, not like this thirst, this death that came by moments. Whatever sin he committed, whatever bad decisions the men accused him of, nothing deserved this. Nothing. But they would die too. What were they guilty of? What had they done to deserve death?

He thought of bargaining for their lives. Would God accept that? Gerardo offered his own life for the lives of his four crewmen. He would give himself up. They were his responsibility, and he would do what was necessary to keep them alive. If it meant his death, fine—kill him but kill him now, right away. Don't let him linger.

That evening, in the darkness of the Penthouse, Pastor told whoever would listen, "No one beats God because God is the most evil and the most good, the alpha and the omega. He's God and man."

"Shut up. I can't sleep," someone said.

"What do you mean, God and man?" another voice asked.

"He's us," Pastor said.

"What?"

"Every person has God inside . . . and also the devil."

"So?"

"Will you guys shut up?"

"So here we are, like Jesus in the desert, and the devil is tempting us, testing us. God is testing us too. We're all being tested."

"Son of a bitch! Will you guys shut up?"

"Calm down, asshole."

It was quiet for a while, then someone said, "I understand all that, but I still think we're going to die."

Without a word, Pastor roused himself from his corner and climbed out of the hatch. He sat on the deck and looked at the stars.

"Good," said the grumbler below, "go talk to the sky."

The second day without drinking water began the same as the first. One man bailed and the others lay around waiting their turn. If they dozed off and the sound of the bailing slowed or stopped, invariably someone accused the bailer of trying to sink the boat, of cheating, or trying to kill them all. Then the sound resumed and the insults stopped.

With their energies gone, about all they could do was concentrate on breathing and coping with their thickening tongues and narrowing throats. But they still had to bail for four hours each, and this became a trancelike, mechanical chore.

On this morning, Pastor began one of his monologues with a challenge. "Let's fix the rudder," he said in a raspy, barely audible voice.

The others stared at him skeptically.

"What for?" Juan asked.

"Because nothing's going to happen if we don't make it happen. Let's fix the rudder, put up the sail, and go to wherever we might see clouds. Dark clouds. How about it?"

Gerardo nodded and suggested they get started immediately, before their strength left them completely. But Juan said they should save their energies and wait, instead of wasting sweat doing something not really necessary.

Pastor said he'd been thinking about it all night. "It's possible we're going to die, right? Then let's at least die fighting like men, not like cowards. Let's die *fighting* death."

The words snapped them out of their lethargy, and the boat quickly became a scene of men in motion. Gerardo and Juan repaired the rudder, and the others checked and mended parts of the sail. When the tattered blankets and mattress covers were raised, the wind filled them out and the *Cairo* headed west.

Joel sat by the tiller, steering and feeling a renewed sense of purpose. They would run to the clouds. There had to be clouds somewhere. All he wanted to see was a hint of clouds, a speck, a dark line somewhere on the horizon ahead. They all doused themselves with water again and huddled in the shade.

"Let's die *fighting*," Joel said. "I like that. How about that, Boom-Boom? You're the boxer."

Jorge wasn't listening; he was squeezing a toothpaste tube.

"What are you doing?" Joel asked him.

"Maybe it'll take some of the thirst away."

The others watched his expression as he smeared a daub of paste on his tongue and the inside of his mouth. After a few moments of smacking his lips, he told them the toothpaste seemed to help him produce a little saliva. Before long, they all finished the toothpaste, disappointed they hadn't squeezed out more of the saliva-stimulating goo for their cotton-dry mouths.

Several hours later they were listless and silent again. Even in the shade, the heat gripped them to the point of suffocation. If they spoke at all, it was mostly in whispers or in moaning signs or grunts. Depressed and beaten, they felt like failures. The evening was spent in a stupor, each man quietly struggling through his own sense of doom.

On the third day Pastor left the Penthouse just after dawn, climbed on top of the awning, and started to lick the dewy film covering the slick surface. It tasted salty, but he figured it had to be better than seawater. Joel emerged on deck, saw Pastor, and also tried to climb up. But in trying to pull himself up, he broke the gutter on the water-collecting side and had to spend several hours repairing it.

By the afternoon they were all crawling on hands and knees, now and then crying or begging in murmurs for rain. They were dizzy, nauseous, and their stomachs felt heavy. Their bodies ached for water, and though their tongues were engorged so that it was painful to speak, they were still angry enough to curse the sky and sea.

Suddenly Gerardo dropped the sail, waited until a small turtle paddled alongside, then pulled it up and flipped it onto its back. With both hands trembling, he grasped the knife handle and drove the blade deep into the throat and chest cavity. Then he held back the twisting head, put a small bowl under the severed artery, filled it, and began to drink. The blood was thick and difficult to swallow, but it was liquid and it didn't taste salty.

"Anybody else?" Gerardo said, pinching the artery and drawing back. Blood dripped from his face and chest, and he licked his lips with his tongue. "Come on, it's not so bad."

"What for?" Jorge whispered. "I'll just get thirsty again."

Only Pastor was tempted to drink from the turtle. It

wasn't much, and before he slumped back gagging, he thought he could taste bile or vomit. Minutes later the blood that had spilled on the deck and on their bodies had darkened and coagulated into pasty stains and smudges.

For a while Gerardo felt revived, then he crawled back to his spot under the bow deck. He was exhausted from the blood-drinking. He had left the turtle where it died, thinking someone might want to butcher and eat it. But they felt they couldn't swallow blood, let alone meat, so they dumped the turtle overboard.

By now the bailing was reduced to a feeble, slow-motion effort that sometimes required two men to keep the water level from rising inside the boat.

Before sunset Joel was awakened from his stupor by dolphin clicks and squeaks. He'd been stretched out in the awning shade with his head against the side, and now he turned to look at the nearby visitors. Since the boat rode low in the water, Joel's face was less than a foot above the surface. He squinted, trying to locate the dolphins, but instead focused on a school of tuna passing underneath, then trigger and other smaller fish darting into the boat's shadow. Raising his sight, he saw the familiar golden-blue dorados leaping after their usual flying prey. He also saw the dolphins and several turtles, and above, beyond where little white birds swooped and skimmed over the water, he gazed on a giant pink sky and a sunset he thought would be his last.

On the morning of the fourth day without water, the five figures on the drifting hulk could barely move. Bailing had been reduced to only an hour or two for each shift, and the scooping itself had become sporadic. The men had survived bouts of delirium during the night and were now attacked by dizzy spells that left them stretched out and useless.

The sky remained cloudless, but the wind continued to blow from the west. Gerardo, sunk in vague thoughts of failure, hardly paid attention to the sky. He didn't have the strength to catch another turtle, and Pastor considered but didn't attempt another climb onto the awning. Instead, he licked moisture from the outside of the water tank.

No one spoke anything intelligible until someone suggested they prepare themselves to die. With a knowing gesture, referring to something they had foreseen would happen, only the word "die" was clearly pronounced. And as they did on so many occasions when a decision was made, when they said, "Let's do it," the five started their motions. Like glassy-eyed, wounded men, they crawled to their bags and small suitcases, kept below or, in Gerardo's case, in the bow. Mouths open, breathing in gulps, they pulled out their best clothes, which they had saved for the occasion: wrinkled, clean short pants and a clean T-shirt.

They had agreed that if they ever knew they were about to die, they would put on their "dying" clothes. That was the plan. Why should they die naked or in ragged, dirty clothes when they could die wearing something clean? Why not leave this earth in style? And if some ship should find them or if the boat should reach an island, shouldn't they look their best?

After they squirmed into the pants and shirts, they crawled under the awning and lay faceup side by side. Joel held his little bottle with the note at his chest. He glanced at it one more time. It contained the money and the note, and the ring was attached to the top. All in order, ready to be dropped into the water just before his last conscious moment.

The morning sunlight hurt Joel's eyes, and he tried to keep them shut. He touched his companions next to him. He could feel them, elbows sharp, hips hard and bony. . . . No one spoke. There was nothing to say. This is how they had planned it. No one would bail, there would be no arguments. The end would come peacefully, quietly, with some sort of harmony. . . .

Joel still struggled with an aching, searing thirst that went beyond thought. But he knew it would all end soon. One by one, they would stop breathing. They would slip away; they would enter the world of the dead.

16] DREAMS

Lidia:

I told God to control my dreams. If Gerardo was alive, show him to me alive. If he was dead, then let me see him dead. One way or another, I had to know. And from then on I would dream of him alive. I had four or five very clear dreams of him. I'd see him coming home to the house, coming right in, or walking down the street in that strong way of his.

In one of the last dreams I had I saw him coming up the canal in the *Cairo III.* The boat was all dirty and broken and falling apart, but it was still floating. And Gerardo was the only one on board.

"Where are the other men?" I asked him.

At first he wouldn't answer. Then he turned to look at me and said, "They all died. I'm the only one left."

Then I asked him, "Are you alive?"

He looked around, sort of doubting, not really sure. He never did answer me.

I started thinking maybe it's true. He's in trouble and he's trying to tell me what's happened. The other men are dead and he's the last one left.

I didn't say anything to Edith because something like that would kill her. All I could do was pray to my God to protect Gerardo and return him to me alive—however he might be, just return him to me. Crippled, without an

189

arm, whatever, but return him to me. I wanted him back. And if he was dead, I wanted him back dead so I could bury him. Whatever happened, I wanted to know something. I couldn't stand it if I didn't know.

Lidia left her mother's kitchen and crossed the tiny living room to answer the front door. The knock had been weak, so she figured it was the little neighbor girl. She opened the door. "Yes?"

"Doña Lidia, did you hear?" the little girl said.

"What?"

"About the boat. It was on the radio. They found it with three of the men alive."

Lidia suddenly felt weak. "My God!"

"One of the dead men, well . . . His name is Pastor. And the other dead man . . ."

Lidia bent down and clutched the girl's shoulders. "Child, what are you saying? Do you know what you're saying?"

The girl shook her head as if she had made a mistake, then she turned and ran out of the palm-covered front yard. Stunned, Lidia also hurried out the yard, crossed the dusty street, and reached the pay phone outside the grocery store. After borrowing a coin, she called the radio station. She knew the number by heart, having heard it repeated on the air so often. She was thinking at least God had answered her. He'd given her back Gerardo, even though he was dead. Isn't that what the little girl meant? That Gerardo was the other dead man, that there were two and Pastor was one and Gerardo was the other. So God had returned him to her. Isn't that what she wanted? Her husband, dead or alive? Isn't that what she asked for? Well, now she could have him back, now she could bury his body, now she could tell the children—

"May I help you?" the voice on the telephone asked.

Lidia's hand trembled. "The *Cairo Three*," she said hesitantly.

"What?"

"You reported about the boat, the *Cairo Three*—that it was found."

"Just a minute," the voice said, "I'll check."

Lidia fidgeted with the phone cord. A few neighbors who also heard the news gathered around and watched her.

"No, ma'am, we haven't made that report. At no time has anyone at this station made such a report. We're very sorry."

Lidia relaxed. "Oh, that's all right. You don't have to be sorry."

"It must have been a rumor."

"Yes, yes—a big lie."

"Something like that. Rumors, just rumors."

Lidia:

Sometimes the rumors would scare us. When they found the *Cairo*'s net, my little one, José, said the other kids in the neighborhood were telling him that that was his father's hand that got caught in the net. I told him it was another lie and he shouldn't pay attention to people like that. They just want to hurt you and make you sad. People like that start rumors and stories. All lies.

At first I used to tell them that their father was waiting to catch more fish, that he wanted to come back with lots of fish, and that's why he was taking so long. But my older boy could tell—he knew something was not right. So I just told them what I knew. I think they understood. I think they took it all better than I did.

It was so hard. We were living with my parents because we couldn't pay the rent on our own place. I went back to work at the cannery, and this time I scaled fish.

My mom watched the kids. But the job lasted only fifteen days because Charlene got so sick she almost died. She was stopped up with worms and everyone told me to take her to the hospital, but I said, "She's only a year and a half old. If I take her to the hospital, she'll die there." So I gave her home medicines and took her to a healer. He used garlic and milk, rubbed her stomach a lot, and little by little she started getting well.

Then I got sick. Stomachaches and headaches for weeks. I was useless, always in pain and depressed, and all the time worrying about Gerardo. Then in May I started getting better, and by the end of the month I told my mom that I could work at home if I had a sewing machine. So she got together some money she'd saved and made a down payment on one of those foot-pedal kind of sewing machines. And when I got it, I started making clothes. I told her I'd pay her back as soon as Gerardo came home and started earning money. But I don't think she believed me—that he was coming back. I meant it, though. I believed God would return him to me. Like I said, dead or alive.

Edith also heard rumors that the boat had been found, either washed up on the Nicaraguan coast, or found at sea, or discovered in pieces on some island beach. She ignored the stories as much as she could, believing only in the spiritist's words that the men were still alive, and in her mother's and her own dreams about Joel, dreams that showed him thin and weak but alive. In Edith's own dreams, Joel appeared in the same condition.

To cheer up her daughter, Alicia encouraged Edith and the girls to go out to the movie theater or to the beach—anything to distract themselves. Once she even took them to a carnival with mechanical rides and a bullfight with clowns. The girls had fun, but Edith became more depressed than usual and left early by herself. She said she felt guilty because she was eating and trying to enjoy herself while her husband was probably dying of hunger and thirst.

By May Edith had given up on the chance the coast guard might help find the men. She no longer called the station or stopped by in person. Leaving her children with her mother or mother-in-law, who now lived with her, she took to the streets to sell clothes, watches, and jewelry for a local wholesaler. With her goods in bags, she spent many days walking door-to-door to selected clients, earning enough to buy food for the family.

Now and then she traveled to San José to visit Victor Monge at the Foreign Relations Ministry or her contacts at several newspaper offices and radio stations. By asking for recent government information and by keeping the story alive among journalists, Edith felt she was doing something positive. If nothing else, such trips usually lifted her spirits, since people like Monge were always encouraging.

Once, around noon, she and Lidia appeared unannounced at his office as he was about to leave.

"It'll just take a minute," Edith said as he showed them in. He had already told them he had no news one way or another to give them.

"This is something my mother-in-law told me," Edith began. "I don't know if it's from a dream or what, but she thinks the men have reached Tahiti."

The man in the dapper gray suit raised his eyebrows, then rose from behind his desk and stepped across the room to the wall map of the world. The women followed. He located the island about five thousand miles from Central America, and it looked almost as far away as Hawaii, only south of the equator instead of north.

"It's a very long distance, but it's possible," Monge

said, and mentioned the voyage of Thor Heyerdahl's balsa raft, *Kon-Tiki*, from Peru to Polynesia.

He explained that the trade winds and currents south of the equator also moved from the east to the west, the same as they did north of the equator. "Now if the *Cairo* somehow had gone far enough south, the men conceivably could have drifted toward Tahiti. I won't say they couldn't do this."

After studying the map for a while longer, he returned to his desk and told the women that the ministry had no direct communication with Tahiti, but he would ask the Costa Rican consulate in Hawaii to somehow try to contact the island. "That's about all I can do. Whatever I find out, you'll be the first to know."

Edith and Lidia thanked him, and as always he told them not to give up hope.

"Never," they replied at once.

After several days, when there was no news of the *Cairo*'s Tahitian arrival, the women's briefly bolstered spirits again fell to a depressed, gloomy level. Edith visited the spiritist and was reassured the men were still alive but were now struggling even more than before. Reading his scribbled words, which he said he received telepathically, the man told her the men continued at sea. There was no mention of Tahiti.

After awaking early on the morning of June 1, Edith told her mother-in-law she was going to fast and pray by herself in her bedroom. She would not eat or even drink water for most of the day. She kissed her daughters, closed the door, then knelt on the wooden floor by her bed. Next to her hands were a bible and an old thin blanket of Joel's, which she folded and unfolded over and over, crying and praying at the same time.

As the hours passed, Edith became thirsty, and soon

she sensed something she had felt before—that the older crewman, Juan, was sick and in pain. It was a feeling she had mentioned before to her mother, but now the feeling was stronger.

She tried to envision Joel, yet all she could muster were memories of herself in his arms, of their promises to each other, of the family walking in the street and him with one of the girls on his shoulders.

With her hand on the bible, she asked God to be directed to a passage that would console her. The part that came to mind was about how Lazarus was raised from the dead after his sisters Martha and Mary pleaded that he be resurrected.

As Edith read the passage, she started thinking that her faith was weakening and that maybe she doubted Joel was still alive. That's why she was led to read about resurrection. Joel's body, like Lazarus' body, was lifeless and rotting, and now only a miracle could bring him back to life.

Her last words before she finished fasting were, "Please, Lord, give me the strength not to lose hope."

After Edith's fast, both she and Lidia suddenly became serene and confident in their daily lives. With Edith, the change occurred during her meditation in the bedroom.

But in Lidia's case, the transformation happened one evening, also in early June, while she was reciting the rosary in a group at the home of the *Cairo*'s owner. She had been weepy most of the day and now could not control her tears. The crying embarrassed her, but the more she tried to stop, the more she cried. Her world had disintegrated, she thought, and the only way out was to regain her composure—at least for the sake of her children. Lidia, too, felt she was losing her faith, her hope that Gerardo and the others were still alive.

Halfway through the rosary, she stopped. Others in

the room continued their prayers. Lidia, barely aware of their murmuring, wiped her face clean of tears and made one request. "Give me back my faith," she said, and immediately felt at peace, her mind at rest.

17] RAIN

June 4:

In the haze between daydreaming and dozing, Gerardo realized the bailing had stopped. It was sometime in the afternoon and he lay faceup under the awning, staring dumbly at a dorado flash over the swells chasing its usual flying prey. He listened for the rhythmic, sloshing sound of scooping and spilling, but all he heard was the raspy, shallow breathing of the three prostrate figures stretched out on the deck next to him.

When he last looked, Juan had been bailing. He figured the old man was resting or had finished his shift. Or maybe he had just given up. After all, why keep the boat afloat when it looked like they were going to die anyway? What did it matter whether they died of thirst or sank in the water to be eaten by sharks?

So Gerardo waited for the sound to resume. He didn't turn to look at Juan or to see what had happened, concentrating only on the monotonous motion of the water, thinking the end would be a slow, crowding out of all light, on his back, eyes closed, unable to move, his ache for moisture now a monstrous weight that was crushing his chest. Gerardo remembered his mother's last moments, dying young and painfully from any of three or four causes, no one knew for sure. He closed his eyes, trying to shake the image, trying to think only of the present, remembering his vow to himself not to go crazy by thinking of his past. Surviving the present was all that mattered. He peeked at the horizon and wondered if the tiny dark shapes he saw when the boat rose up might be clouds. But so what? They had teased and tortured him before—why would they be friendly now?

Finally Gerardo heard a short groan, which was Juan's signal that he had finished his shift and that it was now Gerardo's turn. Tongues had become so swollen that hardly anyone had spoken today. Mostly the men communicated with grunts, groans, and gestures.

Rousing himself, Gerardo sat up and crawled over his companions toward the bailing spot in the deep part of the boat's middle. He and Juan traded places in silence. The dark, heavy-browed man with the matted hair was still wearing his best T-shirt and short pants; they were all wearing their "death" suits, but his was wet because he had doused himself with seawater. Gerardo noticed Juan was also drinking seawater, having trouble swallowing sips from the cup he now held to his lips. Gerardo had tried seawater himself, but it was bitter and made him want to retch.

He poured some over himself, then started bailing. Now and then he glanced at Juan, who was slumped with his eyes closed next to the other three. Gerardo felt it wouldn't be long before the old man would no longer be able to bail, would just lie there and eventually stop moving and breathing. It would happen to all of them, so it didn't matter who went first. Juan and Pastor no longer climbed onto the awning to lick the greasy, dirty moisture collected on the surface; either they didn't have the strength or they had given up on how much good it did them.

And today no one slipped overboard to cool off. Yesterday they paddled around next to the boat, feeling

refreshed from the sting of the wind and saltwater on
their bodies.

Gerardo thought of catching another turtle for its blood,
but he hardly had the strength to bail, let alone heft a
hundred-pound turtle out of the water. The blood had
filled him like thick, warm milk; it was painful to swallow
but at least it wet his blistered lips and fat, chalky tongue.

He bailed, and as the minutes passed, he became dizzy
and his vision blurred. He wanted desperately to lie
down with the others. He controlled the urge by concentrating all his strength and attention on fighting the leaks,
fighting the water filling the boat. He couldn't plug the
leaks anymore, couldn't keep the sea out, so his struggle
became a race between the ocean and himself. He knew
he would lose the race, but it would be worse to lose by
surrendering. His life was his own and he refused to give
it up just by lying down. The others might stop, but he
wouldn't. He would not stop.

Propelled by an angry stubbornness, Gerardo now fought
through the dizziness, the weakness, the endless, suffocating thirst. He thought only of bailing, of emptying the
boat. Lift the water, pour it out, lift, pour, lift, pour.
Soon he forced himself into a mesmerizing chain of slow,
regular movements. He glanced at the watch fixed to a
wooden plank next to the Penthouse. He would not stop.
Even if it killed him, he would reach the end of his shift.

As the sun set on their fourth day of thirst, Gerardo's
will to live apparently grew stronger. The small surge of
determination, which was also felt at times by the others,
may have been sparked or helped along by the bailing
activity itself. This was still something they did without
question, no matter how miserable and listless they were.
Bailing now drained them of energy, but it roused them
from a potentially fatal inertia, keeping them awake and
limber.

But the accounts and studies of sea survival indicate the will to survive weakens as thirst increases. A castaway adrift in the tropics can survive up to seven or eight days without water. The *Cairo* five, given their latitude of about twelve degrees north of the equator, were probably enduring daytime shade temperatures in the eighties and nineties. This meant they might live another several days before they died of dehydration and, if they drank a lot from the ocean, seawater poisoning.

Delirium and unconsciousness usually precede such a death. But as darkness enveloped the *Cairo*, no one had yet lost his mind and everyone could still crawl across the deck to bail.

About ten-thirty that night they felt the first drops. They squirmed out from under the awning, mouths open to the black, starless sky. The sprinkle splashed over their faces and cracked lips, running over eyes, gums, tongues, trickling life down their throats and into their bodies. After a few moments the sprinkle thickened to a shower. Soon the rain was washing away weeks of grime from the awning roof, and the men struggled to hold their plastic jugs to catch the runoff at the bottom of the funnel. Possessed by a frenzied, overwhelming urge to drink, the men started gulping as much as they could of the salty, acidlike water. Moaning with a mixture of pain and joy, they tilted their heads so the water could run over bloated tongues and into swollen, sore throats.

The shower lasted about ten minutes, which was enough time for the men to slake their thirst and collect a half-gallon or so of brackish water. After it stopped, Juan and Pastor again climbed on the roof to lick the moisture that remained on the surface.

"I knew it would rain," Jorge said slowly. They were waiting, faces turned up. "I just knew it."

"That's not what you said yesterday," someone whispered in the dark.

"Today was different."

"Thank God."

"Yes!" Juan wheezed. "Exactly! Thank God . . . oh, thank God."

June 5:

At sunrise, they were revived but wary. They had spent the night waiting, bailing, and sleeping, and now they could see a faraway line of rain clouds to the south. Were the showers leaving them? Was that what had brought them ten minutes of relief, only to let them linger on a few more days? The sky above them wasn't quite clear, and they couldn't decide if clouds were forming or not. It all appeared hazy in the early-morning light.

Someone suggested they raise the sail and try to head south toward the clouds. But they were weak. The blanket and vinyl patches that made up the sail had to be tightened and mended with pieces of wire and rope threads. Gerardo started checking the rudder and someone else began inspecting the sail before they raised it. Suddenly every motion required intense concentration and a tremendous physical effort. They were all extremely thirsty again.

"Let's finish the water," Joel said, raising the opaque plastic jug, half-filled with dark water.

Pastor peered into the jug. "Looks like chocolate."

Joel, the elected keeper and dispenser of the water, poured out the amounts in the waiting cups and bowls. Ignoring the taste of grime, grease, and salt, they drank the awful liquid quickly but carefully. Not a drop should spill.

Afterward, they again became listless and glassy-eyed.

Turtles came close, sometimes raising their heads to observe the motionless figures under the awning, bump the boat, maybe dip underneath the hull, then paddle away. Occasionally sharks approached, along with the usual schools of tuna and dorado. Nothing around the boat appeared to have changed. Even Scarface, his reddish gash still visible along the left side of his head and body, kept them company, but always at a twenty- or thirty-yard distance.

Then a huge, dark shadow swept over the boat. This time it rained hard from the beginning. The sea turned strangely calm, and the water poured from the clouds in hard, vertical sheets. The five men tried to emit whoops and cheers, but all they could produce were spasms of raspy, whispered croaks. As the runoff coursed into the gutter and down their makeshift spout, they channeled the water into their own small containers, then into the forty-five-gallon main tank. By the time the brief squall left them, they were sated and had collected seven gallons of drinking water.

Their mouths still felt thick and their bodies withered and weak, but for the first time in many days they moved spontaneously to do something. They raised the sail, swung the boom around, and caught a light westerly breeze. Everyone agreed the rain looked as if it came from the south, so the waddling little vessel soon struck out under a tiny sail on a 180-degree course. They kept this direction throughout the day, but the distant, billowy thunderheads hardly seemed any closer.

Gerardo and Pastor were the first to resume eating. It wasn't much—some bits of turtle meat leftover from a previous kill—but they managed to keep it down. One by one the others also began chewing small pieces of meat, tentatively at first, like babies trying solid food for the first time, then more quickly once their mouths and throats grew used to the process.

By the afternoon the men realized they might not die, after all. The weather had repeatedly deceived them, but this time it had rained twice in two days, so maybe their luck was changing. Why would the rain appear just as they were approaching death? Had they passed some grand, celestial test? Or were they fated to survive only a while longer, their water gone, the boat sunk?

Joel wasn't taking any chances. He suggested they limit themselves to three-day rations of one gallon per man. This way the seven gallons they had collected in the morning would last them at least four days. No one objected, and Joel carefully filled the five capped containers each man kept for himself.

June 6:
No rain. They caught and ate fish, and they kept sailing straight south.

June 7:
No rain. The swells and waves had increased in height but weren't high enough to swamp the boat. The men continued eating and kept a careful eye on everyone else's individual water ration. About a quart remained for each man at the end of the second day of rationing.

June 8:
It rained hard all day, starting in the early morning and continuing long after sunset. They filled the forty-five-gallon main tank, a seven-gallon reserve tank, a rinsed-out, twelve-gallon auxiliary diesel tank, and the smaller containers belonging to each of the men. All told, they had close to seventy gallons of water stored, enough for two or three weeks if they rationed carefully.

June 9:
They dropped the sail and concentrated on fishing and catching turtles. As they ate, they regained their strength.

Joel unzipped his athletic bag and put away the bottle with the love note to his wife. The high-school ring was still attached, and the money and note were left inside. Gerardo now praised the wind and clouds. Pastor resumed singing. Juan was eager to help cut up the catch. And enfeebled Jorge pulled himself upright by the awning posts and took his first puppetlike steps in more than a week. His knee joints, always painful, were now only an irritating distraction. They all had their aches and cuts and sores, but water and plenty of meat helped the men heal and gave them hope.

At about ten-to-twelve degrees latitude north of the equator, the little rainfall the men of the *Cairo* encountered was so far within the normal precipitation range for the February-to-June period. If they had been several hundred miles farther south, they probably would have found more rain. But by June the usual equatorial band of storms was already moving north, and this is most likely what occurred and why the men finally drank their fill.

June 14:

After drifting for five days under mostly clear skies, the men were bailing faster. The leaks had become larger, and plugging and packing them had become almost impossible, especially the big hole that had grown around the loose keel screw beneath the bow.

The men were stronger, but they hadn't forgotten the agony of their four-day thirst. They kept to strict rationing, and though they drank whenever they wanted, Joel always dispensed the amounts, usually with the others looking on.

Eating was a different matter. Whenever a catch was made, they worked together like a well-oiled machine. Everyone had a role—hauling, killing, slicing, washing—

and the turtle, shark, dorado, triggerfish, or whatever they pulled aboard was quickly transformed into bite-size morsels of meat and split pieces of bone marrow. Nothing edible was wasted, and anything left over was saved for later. With their few hooks, two spears, one gaff, two knives, and a small machete, they became an efficient production-line team. By now they knew each other's talents and limitations so well that arguments were few and usually settled with a shrug or a nod.

On this day, a Wednesday, about eleven in the morning, a small shark struck Joel's line. After a brief struggle, he pulled it close to the boat, gaffed it, and yanked the twisting creature up and onto the deck. Several hours later, they had finished their feast. Sated, they spent most of the afternoon sleeping, if they weren't bailing. Joel had thrown another baited hook and line into the water and was dozing next to the Penthouse hatch cover when he felt a sharp jerk on the line. He looked over the side into the water.

"Another shark," Joel said, almost casually.

The other men hardly stirred. They knew Joel would ask for help when and if he needed it. For five or ten minutes he was so absorbed in bringing up the shark that he never raised his head, never looked up at the surrounding water, never noticed what was approaching— not until he was about to gaff the shark.

It was late afternoon, the *Cairo* pitched in three- to four-foot seas, and a swash of sunlight shimmered across the plain of countless white-tipped waves.

18] RESCUE

At four-forty-five in the afternoon, June 14, Fumiya Sato was about to finish his watch on the bridge of the 409-ton *Kinei Maru 128*, a Japanese tuna-fishing ship. The twenty-two-year-old engineer was peering through the thick glass at the aprons of foam breaking on the swells. The lowering sunlight slanted into the room, and Sato shielded his eyes with one hand. Less than three weeks out of its home port of Kesennuma, north of Tokyo, the sleek, modern vessel was on its maiden voyage and headed toward fishing grounds in the eastern Pacific. Half of the twenty-man crew were natives of Kesennuma, which in 1978 was proclaimed the sister city of Puntarenas, Costa Rica.

When Sato first glimpsed the faraway, dark object bobbing on the swells, he thought it might be an abandoned or derelict boat, or a log—the sun's reflection on the water made it difficult to see clearly. He raised the binoculars and immediately spotted two figures waving frantically in the *Kinei Maru*'s direction. Sato notified the captain, Tatsuo Koyama, who also studied the decrepit little boat. Koyama then conferred with the ship's other senior officer, Fishing Master Osao Kumagai. They decided to cut the engine speed, change course, and approach their strange discovery.

The ship was now about 550 miles southeast of Honolulu—

or 10°-18′ degrees latitude north, 151°-34′ degrees longitude west.

Fumiya Sato:

At first it was all a mystery. When we came closer to the boat, four men were waving their hands. Another man was bailing. I thought it was a wrecked boat when I saw them at a close distance, but I wasn't sure because they looked fine. Their language sounded like Spanish, their faces and body type were different from Europeans or Americans, and the kind of boat they had was unfamiliar to us, quite different from a yacht. The hull was wooden and looked in very poor condition. Even the name of the country they shouted at us didn't come to mind at first. Costa Rica? Where was that? And on what island around here did they speak Spanish? I couldn't think of any. Later on, I found out the answers to these and other questions about the men and their boat.

Captain Koyama and Fishing Master Kumagai initially were wary of the odd craft and its desperate-looking passengers. Who were they? Where were they from? What happened to them? What were they shouting? While the *Kinei Maru* idled about fifty yards from the boat, the two officers decided to call the ship's agent in Honolulu and ask him to contact the U.S. Coast Guard. Maybe they had information on the boat. They also radioed their home office in Japan to explain the situation. But while they waited for an answer, they noticed the clouds were thickening. It would soon be dark, and if the men were actually shipwrecked and had to be rescued, they should be taken aboard right away, while there was still light. If the officers waited much longer, they might have to carry out a rescue operation at night, and that would be difficult and dangerous.

The fishing master, a fifty-eight-year-old veteran with decades of experience in the Pacific, looked through the binoculars one more time, then shrugged. "So let's bring one of them up—see what he has to say."

Joel was the first to see the fishing ship. He was holding on to the rope stretched between two of the awning posts, about to gaff the shark he'd just caught. That's when he glanced up and saw the long white hull and superstructure of the *Kinei Maru* about a half-mile away. "Son of a bitch," he yelled. "A ship! How did we miss it?"

Angry at himself and the others for not checking the horizon from time to time, Joel continued yelling about how the ship was already passing them and it was because of their own laziness that no one had seen it sooner.

Pastor and Juan climbed on the awning and started waving their arms and shouting for help. The others shouted and waved too, but with the swells as high as they were, the two men on the roof had the best chance of attracting attention.

"It's turning," Gerardo cried out from the bow.

The men kept up the commotion as the ship started its wide, slow turn. Joel remembered his hooked shark and hurriedly tied the line to a post. A leftover dorsal fin from their midday feast hung under the awning, and in the water more sharks circled the boat. For some reason there were plenty of sharks today, more than enough. Joel wished they would go away; they were no longer needed as food.

The ship stopped about forty or fifty yards away from the *Cairo*. The five could see crewmen on the main deck gesturing to them and shouting something unintelligible.

"Chinese," Pastor said.

"Again," Joel added, thinking of their disastrous encounter with the *Clipper* oil tanker.

"They want us to swim across," Gerardo said.

Joel studied the water. The sharks appeared to have gone—or were lurking somewhere beneath the surface. "Seems far, but I suppose it's the only way."

For a long while the *Cairo* five fretted, pleading with the figures standing by the rail. Suddenly a line shot out from the ship and dropped across the middle of the boat. A lifesaver had been attached to the end, and the men rushed to yank it in. From the gestures of the Japanese crew, the Costa Ricans guessed their saviors first wanted to pull only one man to the ship. Without much discussion, Joel was chosen to be the group's interpreter and the first one across.

Helped by the others, he wrapped the ship's line around himself, then clutched the lifesaver to the back of his thighs as he was lowered into the water. He shifted his weight so that he was now sitting on the tire-shaped object.

"Don't let them see the whites of your feet," Pastor reminded him. He was referring to the sharks' supposed attraction to the light-colored soles of human feet. Gerardo added that he couldn't see any sharks.

"Maybe the ship's engine scared them away," Joel said, and he signaled to be pulled across. The water felt warm on his bare legs, but he was shivering, thinking only of the sharks. He had suffered too much, traveled too far, waited too long for this moment. The image of himself being attacked by sharks just before he could be pulled out filled him with dread. He started paddling hard with his hands, crying out to the men ahead, "Faster! Faster!" even though he was sure they didn't understand him.

Though the distance was about the width of a soccer field, the haul across to the *Kinei Maru* seemed interminable. He wished he could fly, imagined himself skimming across the water, and prayed the sharks beneath him would ignore all his splashing.

When Joel reached the ship, he grabbed the flexible ladder hanging over the side, freed himself of the lifesaver, and started up.

Fishing Master Osao Kumagai:
By now I was sure they were shipwrecked. We threw over a life buoy to them and took one of the men onto our boat. We tried to communicate using body language, and from his gestures and writing I figured this man— Joel Omar González Rivera—that he and his companions wanted to be rescued, even if they had to abandon their boat. At the time he kept holding up one hand, or five fingers. I thought it meant five days. But that was inconsistent with the boat's condition and the surrounding facts. Later I understood he meant five months. They were adrift on the ocean for five months.

The four on board cheered when Joel made it safely across, then they waited until he finished explaining who they were and what had happened to them.

"They'll have to kill him if they want to get him off," Jorge said.

"What about us?" Juan asked. He was nervous and still queasy from stomach pangs he suffered the night before.

"Don't worry," Gerardo said, "they'll take all of us. They wouldn't save only one."

They waited a while longer, then the line was thrown out again. Gerardo caught it.

"That's it, papa," Joel cried. "Grab it and pull yourself across. We're going home!"

The four hesitated, scanning the water near the boat. Pastor and Juan were the most fearful of jumping in, but

Gerardo and Jorge were eager to get across. From the ship Joel again told them to jump in the way he did, one by one. By now, though, the ship's drift and the current had brought the two vessels to within twenty yards of each other. Pulling on the line brought them even closer, until Gerardo plunged in at the top of a swell and dog-paddled across. After a few moments Jorge caught the line and also jumped in.

Juan, meanwhile, had been scurrying around collecting the bags and little suitcases they had stored in the icebox and bow. Joel repeatedly yelled down to Juan to tie their luggage together with the ship's line. Besides their identification cards, their personal belongings mostly included a few pieces of clothing and their shoes, which they hadn't worn since they left Puntarenas nearly five months ago. Joel had also filled his zippered bag with reminders of the trip—the boat's compass, a few tools, and the bottle with the note to Edith.

When the *Cairo*'s stern edged up to the *Kinei Maru*, Juan, then Pastor crossed over to the ship without having to wet their feet.

As Pastor pushed away, the empty, worm-eaten craft pitched back slightly, then someone on the deck pushed the boat away with a shove. The *Cairo* looked pathetic: blood, oil, rust, algae, and barnacles had stained the once-white hull and red trim; a stumpy, nailed-together mast rose above a dark, empty shell saturated with the stench of five men in long confinement; and the Costa Rican flag, its colors bleached away by the sun, drooped in tatters from its stick above the awning.

For several minutes the rescued men held on to the deck rail, watching their dilapidated home for the past five months rock its way toward the ship's stern, then drift off, wallowing amid the white-peaked waves.

"Damn rotten prison," Pastor muttered. "Go on, go away, go to hell."

Gerardo spoke, "I give it four hours, maybe three, before it sinks."

"Good," Pastor said, and was about to turn away when he slapped his forehead and cried out, "I forgot the Bic!"

"Too late now."

Upset with himself, Pastor resumed cursing the boat and shaking his head.

Above them, on a higher deck, a crewman pointed a video camera at the *Cairo III*, now and then catching jerky glimpses of the dark and grizzled survivors. In one pan of the deck, a barefoot, shirtless Juan appeared looking stunned and quizzical. Moments later, off camera, Juan was seen crying.

By now the five knew their rescuers were Japanese, not Chinese, since several of the ship's crew knew a few words in Spanish and someone had a Spanish-Japanese dictionary. The survivors were taken inside to the showers and given soap, shampoo, razors, cologne, toothpaste, toothbrushes, and towels. They were also given clean shirts, underwear, and pants.

"I can't believe it, I can't believe it," Joel said, holding the soap to his nose, breathing deeply, smiling. "Incredible—everything, just incredible."

For a long while the men stayed under the hot shower streams, scrubbing and soaping themselves, rinsing off and soaping, again and again. They couldn't have dreamed up better, more friendly hosts. They'd been told they were going to Honolulu, and now someone sang Joel's favorite refrain about the unparalleled beauties of Hawaii, and they all laughed.

When dinner was enthusiastically offered to them, they accepted, even though they still felt full from their earlier meal of shark. They didn't want to appear unappreciative, thinking the Japanese expected them to behave like starving men. So that evening the survivors ate to the bursting point. They ate until they became dizzy and nauseous. Joel even wanted to ask for Alka Seltzer but kept quiet. If he asked, he'd insult the cook, who was happy serving them course after course.

Shinji Iwatsuki, ship's cook:
I was making dinner when they were found and rescued. The first thing I did was make them take a shower. While they were taking a shower, I asked five or six of the crew to offer them clothes to change into. I myself took out one set—T-shirt, pants, and shorts—to give them. Each of the rescued men thanked us and then I served them dinner. They had a good appetite and ate everything I put before them.

That night after they had finished dinner, I spoke to the eldest, using a little of the Spanish and Italian I know. *"¿Cómo se llama usted?"* I asked.

"Juan," he answered.

"Edad?"

"Cuarenta y siete."

"Bambino cuánto?"

"Seis."

He was standing outside at the stern, looking at the sea and holding his hands to his chest, repeatedly saying, *"Muchas gracias, muchas gracias."* I was very touched when I saw the tears running down from his eyes.

The first night none of them slept. I think they were too excited. I got up before dawn and went down to the kitchen to prepare breakfast. But before I did that, I washed my face, then went outside on the stern deck to throw away some garbage. That's when I found them, all five, on their knees facing the rising sun, praying and giving thanks for being saved.

After they finished breakfast, we asked them what had

happened to them. From what we could understand, they were pulled by a big fish that made a hole in the boat and turned it to one side, and then the water came into the engine compartment. Afterward they drifted, every day seeing only sea and sky, drinking rainwater and eating turtles and fish.

I was surprised to see that after five months adrift they weren't weakened but were strong and healthy in body and spirit.

The next night two or three of them stayed awake, and the others slept. The third night all of them slept, probably because they had finally calmed down and had some peace of mind. I know this because every night I went to them frequently.

The day before we entered Honolulu harbor, I prepared a special dinner, wanting them to enjoy their last evening with us. I asked what they wanted to eat and they answered they would like chicken. So I prepared roast chicken, salted roast lobster, mixed fruits, a vegetable salad, egg soup, and rice. They ate everything. Only one of them, Juan, did not eat, saying he had a headache. We were worried about him and gave him some medicine.

He had a high temperature, so we tried to cool him down with ice packs and cold towels. Gradually his temperature came down and he fell asleep, and we were relieved. About two hours later he found me in the kitchen and made a sign over his stomach that he was hungry. I brought out the roast chicken he'd left untouched and he began to eat like a starved man.

Apparently the Japanese misunderstood Gerardo, whom they called the "captainlike" member of the group, when he tried to describe the leaks in the *Cairo*'s hull. They thought he meant a swordfish or marlin had punctured the boat after being caught on a line. Then the big fish dragged them far out to sea. The Japanese also believed only a few men could fit in the boat's icebox and that they ate raw meat during the entire period adrift.

On Friday, June 17, after two days and three nights aboard the Japanese vessel, the five survivors stood on a windy deck in the morning sunlight to record their last words of thanks on video. Puffing a cigarette, Gerardo hardly spoke, Juan couldn't be heard, Joel and Jorge were slightly more expressive, but Pastor, never scarce of words, showered his saviors with streams of gratitude.

After the ship docked at Honolulu's seldom-used Pier 31, coast-guard officials, reporters, the Costa Rican consul, and other well-wishers gathered to hear Gerardo's brief version of their ordeal. "We were never starving," he said. "We never gave up hope because we have a great faith in God and kept praying to return to our families."

Gerardo was the only one of the five who spoke, the others no longer objecting to his leadership. The crew had not forgotten the early mishaps, but they believed Gerardo in his isolated way had suffered as much, if not more, as any of them. However, at the time, only the five survivors, now draped in leis, knew of the original net accident and the two near-rescues. They felt it would be too embarrassing to publicly admit they had failed when the *norte* hit, then failed twice again when they might have been saved.

What they didn't realize was that they had become heroes, having just set a world record for the longest recorded period that anyone has ever survived adrift on the open sea.

"To our knowledge right now," said Lieutenant Bradley Nelson, the coast-guard spokesman on hand, "the longest anyone has survived drifting is four and a half months, and that was during World War Two in the South Atlantic."

Lieutenant Nelson was referring to Poon Lim's 133-day ordeal floating on a raft off the northern coast of Brazil. By comparison, the men of the *Cairo III* survived 142 days, from the time they lost the net and control of the boat, January 25, to their rescue June 14 late in the day, Hawaii time. Surviving on rainwater, fish, and an estimated two hundred turtles, they had crossed four time zones and traveled about forty-five hundred miles. If they had continued another two thousand miles, drifting west with the equatorial current, they would have reached the Marshall Islands in another five or six weeks.

The Fishing Master Kumagai, however, believed the *Cairo* crew would have perished if his ship had not rescued them when it did. This was because a near-hurricane condition was about to hit the area. Kumagai even reported that after the storm a lone American was found dead and adrift in a disabled boat near Johnston Atoll, about a thousand miles northwest of the *Cairo*'s rescue site. The Costa Ricans were headed in that general direction, and they probably would have met with a similar fate.

Before saying their farewells and embracing their rescuers—especially the cook—the five survivors watched Captain Koyama receive a letter of praise from the local coast-guard commander. The letter cited the *Kinei Maru* crew's willingness to help "the fellow mariners who were stranded in the Pacific for almost five months" as being among "the highest traditions of men who sail the sea."

Later, just before noon, the five were taken by military van to Tripler Army Medical Center and admitted for examination by a team of emergency-room doctors. Their translator for the afternoon was Army Staff Sergeant José Rosario, a Puerto Rican teletype clerk.

*   *   *

Sergeant Rosario:

They were amazed that after five months they were still alive. They were waiting for their time to die. They were also amazed that the people in the United States were very hospitable.

I remember one of them saying that after being in the water that long and surviving what they went through, they could never be mean to anyone again. They were just thankful to be alive.

Major Fred Thaler was the attending physician in the emergency room when the survivors arrived.

Major Thaler:

We kept them about three to four hours in ER just to run all the tests and make sure they were doing all right. For what they had been through, they were in superb shape. They really looked good. One had a mouth infection, but the rest of them were fine.

They didn't suffer from exposure because the boat had a shelter or cover. So they weren't terribly exposed. I was expecting them to be sunburned, but that was not the case. They had the cover on the boat and they were actually able to get below.

Truthfully, they didn't seem terribly emaciated. They were a little on the lean side, but I suspect that that might not have been too far from their baseline.

One of the things that you would expect to find in such cases is for them to be lacking in vitamins, or show the first signs of scurvy. But, no, nothing was terribly obvious along those lines. Certainly they had not been eating a lot of fresh fruits and vegetables.

They all looked excellent, were coordinated, and were able to walk very well. Afterward, after the screening tests, after we released them, I remember thinking they just seemed to be in awe of the whole situation.

19] HOME

Sunday night, three days before the men were rescued, Lidia went to bed earlier than usual. She was tired, had put the kids to sleep, and lay under the mosquito netting listening vaguely to the radio sounds of her neighbors and thinking of Gerardo. The air was thick and still, and she felt warmer than usual. But her children seemed fine, their breathing smooth and regular.

Suddenly a breeze pushed through the gauzy window curtains, swept coolly across Lidia's face, and rustled a calendar on the wall. The breeze seemed to relax and soothe her, and she soon fell asleep. That was about nine o'clock.

A half-hour later she was awakened by a voice that spoke close to her ear. The voice whispered, "They've been found." Lidia looked at the clock to check the time, then fell into a deep sleep.

A few doors away, on Wednesday morning, June 15, Edith noticed a black butterfly on the wall at the head of the stairs near her bedroom. Frightened and believing it was an omen of death, she hurried to tell her mother-in-law, who was downstairs with the girls. The two women studied the butterfly.

"It means death, doesn't it?" Edith said.

"No," the older woman said. "Death butterflies are

218

much bigger and they don't have spots. See the little white spots?"

Edith nodded, relieved, then glanced around at the other walls and the ceiling.

"But you know what I saw on the gate outside?" her mother-in-law continued. "Those little birds with the yellow breasts. I saw two of them, and they sang."

Edith remained silent as she started down the stairs. She needed no explanation. It was said that the yellow-breasted birds always arrived in pairs to announce an arrival or a death.

She crossed the small living room to open the front door. Outside, perched on the wrought-iron gate, two birds whistled their warning. It was about nine A.M. and the streets were already busy with people walking by or bumping over the rocks and ruts on their bicycles and motorbikes.

"Doña Edith," a young boy called, his head poked between the gate bars. "Did you hear?"

"Hear what?"

"They found the *Dragón* this morning."

"What?"

The boy started to hurry away. "Near El Salvador . . . they're all alive."

Edith said to herself, "Thank God, they're alive." Then she had the depressing thought that with the *Dragón*'s discovery, they would probably stop any more searches and the *Cairo* would be forgotten for sure. There would be no more efforts to find the two missing boats from Puntarenas. Now that one boat had turned up, people would conclude one miracle was enough. Before returning to the house, Edith looked around for the yellow-breasted birds. They had gone. They had announced an arrival, but had they also signaled death? She felt a moment of envy, then smiled wistfully. At least the families of the rescued men wouldn't have to suffer anymore.

Less than an hour later Edith was busy in the kitchen when she heard the phone ring. The girls were outside playing, and her mother-in-law couldn't answer because she was in the bathroom. Edith wiped her hands dry and hurried across the tile floor toward the old sofa and the telephone.

"Yes?"

"Edith?" asked the voice of the boat owner's brother, Jorge Rohmán.

"Hello, Don Jorge. How are you?"

"Edith, start jumping around."

"What?"

"Start dancing and yelling—the boys have appeared!"

"But—but how can that—"

"It's true, they've been found—alive!"

"You're lying."

"No-no-no."

"But Don Jorge, don't you mean the other boat that was lost, the *Dragón*?"

"No, it's the *Cairo*—near Hawaii—but don't spread it around until we get the official—"

Edith didn't hear the rest of his explanation because she slumped onto the sofa and dropped the receiver. Then her mother-in-law rushed over and picked up the phone.

"What's the matter?" she said into the phone. "This girl's fallen apart."

Jorge Rohmán told her the men had been found alive and well, but before he could give more details, his listener had fallen to her knees. "Thank God, thank God," she kept repeating.

The two women embraced each other for a long moment, then without a word Edith rushed out the front

door, into the street, and ran toward Lidia's place. By
the time she reached the house, Edith's face had lost its
color and she was gasping for breath. She stumbled through
the open doorway and saw Lidia with her mother at the
other side of the room. The two women were next to the
washing machine.

Edith approached. She was crying and trying to speak.
"They . . . they . . . they—"

"What is it?" Lidia asked, alarmed.

"They . . ."

"They what?"

"They found them."

Later, after Lidia and her children ran through the
streets shouting the news, embracing and rejoicing with
everyone they saw, Pastor's wife, Rita, was ironing shirts
in the home of a well-to-do Puntarenas family. In the
past few months she had grown thin, and dark hollows
had appeared around her eyes. Her employer, a pleasant,
optimistic woman, continually reminded her not to give
up hope. But now, after nearly five months since her
husband's disappearance, Rita felt her hope and faith
slipping away.

"Rita! They've found your husband! I just heard the
news." Rita's employer rushed into the room. "Leave
the ironing."

"But . . . but how?" Rita stammered.

"The men are fine."

Nervous, Rita pressed down harder on the iron, moving it faster and faster.

"Rita, go home now—go where you're needed."

Across the mountains, on the Caribbean side of Costa
Rica, Jorge Hernández's father, Francisco, was sweeping
clean the hard-packed ground at the rear of his small

farmhouse. Weak from a gall-bladder operation, he too had begun to lose hope that his youngest and closest son would be found alive. Jorge had helped him build the house and plant the corn and bananas, and together they had watched many baseball games on their little TV.

Francisco looked up when his dog started barking. His pregnant daughter, Matilde, was running along the dirt road that came from the train tracks.

"Papá," she shouted. "The five men—they found them! They found them!"

Moments later, the tall, gaunt-faced man extended a bony hand to his daughter and the two embraced, Francisco whispering, "My son . . . my son."

Two days later in the afternoon, the families of the five survivors watched the first newscasts showing the actual rescue scene taken from the video of a Japanese crewman, followed by shots of the men after they arrived in Honolulu. Edith kept calling the TV station pleading with the news director to show their men again. At first he refused, saying the station had to receive a lot of requests before they would consider a rebroadcast.

"Fine," Edith said, controlling her tears, "you'll get them."

Almost immediately, she, Lidia, the kids, and nearly everyone who showed up to congratulate the women spread out through the barrio, asking people to call the station. That evening the rescue of the *Cairo III* and its crew was rebroadcast half a dozen times on the country's main TV channels.

On Wednesday morning, June 22, shortly after ten, the men finally arrived at San José's Juan Santamaría Airport aboard a Costa Rican Airlines plane. After being examined by doctors in Honolulu, they had been flown first-class to Los Angeles, California, to be interviewed again and to make their connection for their flight home. Tense and exhausted, they were ushered out of the plane just behind a pretty brunette wearing a Miss Costa Rica sash. On the public side of the customs inspection area, the hundreds of people waiting for the five fishermen hardly noticed her.

The survivors, wearing T-shirts with Hawaiian logos, avoided Customs and were quickly escorted into the nearby conference room crowded with reporters, cameras, lighting equipment, government people, and close family members. Joel struggled through the crush of bodies to reach Edith, embraced her, lifted up his youngest daughter, and tried to speak. The other women and children were screaming and crying, on their knees giving thanks, crowding around and struggling to get close to the men. In one corner, Jorge and his father clung to each other, and in the rear of the room, now seated, Juan shielded his eyes from the camera lights with a baseball cap. His eldest son, nineteen years old, sat on his father's lap; the two were openly sobbing.

Minutes later, the rescued five were seated at a long table set with glasses of water and a cluster of microphones. Gerardo, his arms around his three small children, was seated next to Costa Rica's First Lady, Margarita Penón de Arias. Farther along, next to Jorge, was the Security Minister Hernán Garrón, the man who once suggested to Edith that she resign herself to widowhood. He now greeted her as if she had won the lottery.

When the men were asked to speak, they all briefly expressed their gratitude and happiness at returning, then Joel did most of the talking. He described their battle to keep the boat afloat during the initial storm and mentioned their periods of hunger and thirst. "We shared in everything we did," he said, "eating, drinking, bailing, fishing, and sleeping. I think what got us through was staying united, doing things as one."

After the press conference, the men were led out into the main terminal hall where hundreds of boisterous, cheering well-wishers, mostly from Puntarenas, waited to greet them. A huge *Welcome* banner stretched over their heads, and Gerardo was soon raised on shoulders and paraded around and outside the terminal to a waiting line of buses, trucks, cars, and vans. Eventually the caravan of vehicles, horns blaring, loaded up and started toward San José and the neighboring city of Cartago, where the five would kneel at the altar in the Basilica of the Angels to give thanks for their salvation.

By late afternoon the caravan had wound down the Pacific coast slopes to Puntarenas. There, thousands more people—mostly on foot or on bicycles—accompanied the parade around the city. Joel and Juan had slipped away to their homes, complaining of headaches. But Gerardo, Pastor, and Jorge stood on a gated platform truck, waving and throwing kisses to the worshipful crowd of local residents—mostly fishermen themselves, cannery workers, or people connected to the fishing industry. It was the biggest turnout for a mass celebration in the city's history—bigger, people said, than when Puntarenas won a national soccer title.

Time and again the three beaming figures on the truck were hailed as heroes, as lost men miraculously returned from the sea. The parade looped through the city for an hour, then headed back along the peninsula to the Veinte de Noviembre barrio. There, next to the airport strip, a massive street party with a hired band went on through the evening till daylight.

At home, Joel became restless and irritable, harsh in his language, not the gentler person he was when he left five months ago. The squeals of excitement by his four daughters, the crush of all the voices and faces surrounding him since he arrived, even his wife's adoring attention to him—the entire blast of emotions defeated him, bringing on a searing, throbbing pain at the temples.

"I just want to lie down," he told Edith.

She held on to his arm. "The girls won't be sleeping with me anymore."

"I mean alone. I need some peace."

"I'm sorry they're making so much noise. They're just happy you're back."

"I know, but dammit, everything's closing in."

Joel slipped his hand into his athletic bag and fished out the little brown bottle. His ring was tied to the top, and the note and paper money were still inside. "Here. There's something inside for you."

"What is it?"

"Something I wrote for you . . . when I was out there." He was about to continue when he suddenly felt weak. Downstairs, the girls were giggling and yelling. "I've got to lie down."

Edith opened the door and followed him in. He dropped onto the bed and closed his eyes while Edith caressed his forehead with one hand. "All day I used to lie here," she said, "thinking of you, wishing . . . if only you were here, if only you were here. I used to tell the other wives, 'Don't lose faith. If you do, they'll die. If you don't, they'll live.' "

It wasn't until the next morning, after he came out of the shower, that Edith had Joel open the bottle and read the note. They sat on the bed and he squinted at the torn scrap of paper with the block of tiny cramped lines. "Third of March—my beloved," he began, clearing his throat, and read the words he'd written far away but not so long ago.

AFTERWORD

Of the five survivors, only Gerardo Obregón returned to deep-sea fishing after they had been home for several months. Although not yet a captain on another boat, Gerardo still believes fishing is the best and easiest way to make a living. Once stubborn and reserved, he thinks the months adrift softened him into a more open and less obstinate person. Lidia agrees, adding that he now eats anything she serves him.

Joel González drives a delivery truck for the bakery he runs at the rear of his house. Like the others, he insists the hardships at sea taught him to love life and his family more than ever before.

True to his dream, Pastor López works as a clam-digger around the mangroves near Puntarenas, and he doesn't think he'll ever return to serious ocean-fishing.

Jorge Hernández helps his father run the family farm in the interior near the town of Río Frío.

And Juan Bolívar, feeling reborn, is back to doing odd jobs on land and spends a lot of his time with his children.

"We'll never forget the trip," Gerardo says. "You don't forget something like that, something that almost killed you. Nowadays I take everything in stride, live with the basics, appreciate every moment of life. I think I know what it's all about."

226

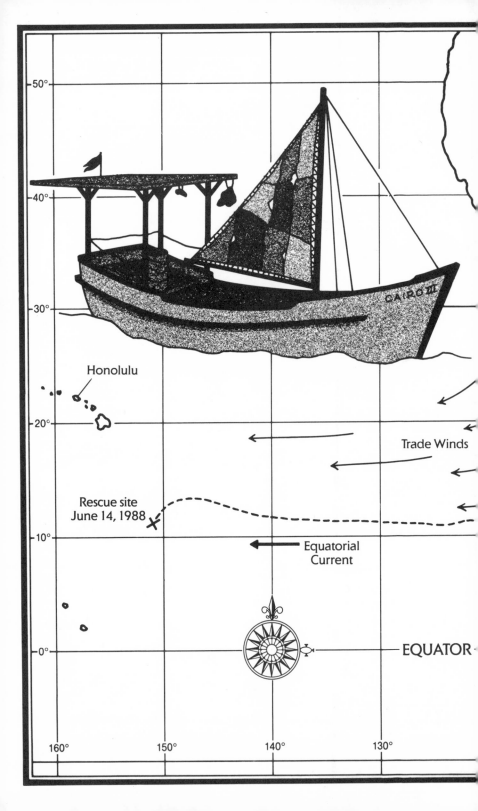

-50°

-40°

-30°

Honolulu

-20°

Trade Winds

Rescue site
June 14, 1988

Equatorial
Current

-10°

EQUATOR

160°   150°   140°   130°